# DISCOVERING YELLOWSTONE WOLVES

## WATCHER'S GUIDE

# DISCOVERING YELLOWSTONE WOLVES

## *WATCHER'S GUIDE*

James C. Halfpenny, Ph.D.
Diann Thompson, B.S.N.

In Collaboration with

**Yellowstone Center for Resources
Yellowstone National Park**

1996

A Naturalist's World / Gardiner, MT

Published May 21, 1996

© by **James C. Halfpenny and Diann Thompson**

All rights reserved. No part of this book may be reproduced in any form or by any electronic or mechanical means, including information storage and retrieval systems, without written permission from the authors.

First Edition    1  2  3  4  5  6  7  8  9

Published in the United States by

**A Naturalist's World**
**(406) 848-9458**
**PO Box 989**
**Gardiner, MT 59030**

## MADE IN MONTANA

**Some Funds from the sale of this book will be donated to Yellowstone Wolf Restoration.**

**Cover and Color Pages:** The background for the cover and color pages grades from gray to yellow representing thermal alteration of Yellowstone's volcanic rhyolite rock. Under intense heat and pressure, the gray volcanic material transforms to the yellow rock so well exhibited in the Grand Canyon of the Yellowstone.

**Front Cover:** Wolf ~ 10 was the first of the translocated wolves to be lost from the Yellowstone project. He was shot about April 26, 1995 near Red Lodge, Montana. Photograph by Barry O'Neill.

**Back Cover:** The first wolf returns to Yellowstone National Park on January 12, 1996 carried by Secretary of Interior Bruce Babbit, Director of Fish and Wildlife Service Mollie Beattie, Yellowstone Wolf Restoration Project Leader Mike Phillips, Yellowstone Park Superintendent, Mike Finley, and Acting Facilities Manager Jim Evanoff.

# TABLE OF CONTENTS

To See a Wolf . . . . . . . . . . . . . . . . . . 1
Dedication  . . . . . . . . . . . . . . . . . 2
Viewing Wolves . . . . . . . . . . . . . . . . 3
    Safety and Etiquette . . . . . . . . . . . . . . 3
    The Best Place and Time . . . . . . . . . . . 4
Wolves of Yellowstone . . . . . . . . . . . . 5
    Acclimation Pens and Release Sites . . . . . . 5
    Naming Wolves and Packs . . . . . . . . . . 6
Getting to Know Your Wolves . . . . . . . . 7
    Class of 1995 . . . . . . . . . . . . . . . . . . 8
        Crystal Creek Pack . . . . . . . . . . . . . . 8
        Leopold Pack . . . . . . . . . . . . . . . . . 9
        Rose Creek Pack . . . . . . . . . . . . . . 10
        Soda Butte Pack . . . . . . . . . . . . . . . 11
    Class of 1996 . . . . . . . . . . . . . . . . . 15
        Chief Joseph Pack . . . . . . . . . . . . . . 15
        Druid Peak Pack . . . . . . . . . . . . . . 16
        Lone Star Pack . . . . . . . . . . . . . . . 16
        Nez Perce Pack . . . . . . . . . . . . . . . 17
    In Memorial . . . . . . . . . . . . . . . . . . 20
How to Identify a Wolf . . . . . . . . . . . 22
    Wolves . . . . . . . . . . . . . . . . . . . . . 22
    Coyotes . . . . . . . . . . . . . . . . . . . . 24
    Telling Yellowstone's Canines Apart . . . . 25
About Wolves . . . . . . . . . . . . . . . . . 30
    Evolution . . . . . . . . . . . . . . . . . . . 30
    Taxonomy . . . . . . . . . . . . . . . . . . . 31
    Biology and Ecology . . . . . . . . . . . . . 33
    Behavior . . . . . . . . . . . . . . . . . . . . 41
Wolf Restoration . . . . . . . . . . . . . . . . 45
    History . . . . . . . . . . . . . . . . . . . . . 45
    Process . . . . . . . . . . . . . . . . . . . . . 47
    Origins . . . . . . . . . . . . . . . . . . . . . 48
    Soft versus Hard Release . . . . . . . . . . 49
    Chronology . . . . . . . . . . . . . . . . . . 51
    Who's Who . . . . . . . . . . . . . . . . . . 53
From Project Leader, Mike Phillips . . . 55
Learning about Wolves . . . . . . . . . . . . 56

A Watcher's Guide for 1997 . . . . . . . . 62

# ACKNOWLEDGEMENTS

Many people have helped with this project from formative thought processes, to field time, to editorial comments, to logistical support, and in other important aspects. We wish to especially thank Ed Bangs, Bob Barber, Norm Bishop, Stacey Churchwell, Lynn Coy, Steve Fritz, Brad Garfield, Mark Johnson, Marsha Karle, Bob Landis, Cheryl Matthews, Elizabeth Murray, Diane Papineau, Belinda Peck, Lance Peck, Barry O'Neill, LuRay Parker, Mike Phillips, Drew Ross, Doug Smith, Jim Peaco, and John Varley for their help.

Others, including Renee Askins, Wayne Brewster, Bob Crabtree, Renee Evanoff, Hank Fischer, Deb Guernsey, John Mack, Dan MacNulty, Carrie Schaefer, J. Douglas Smith, Pat Tucker, Nathan Varley, Bruce Weide, and Alice Whitlaw, provided help over the longer run and are equally appreciated.

There are many who remain out of sight of the public that are helping to make Wolf Restoration work. We wish to say thanks to these folks including the staff of Yellowstone National Park, the Wolf Guards, and other Wolf Volunteers.

To all our students, especially those from the Yellowstone Institute Wolf Classes and to Pam Gontz and Don Nelson, who make the Institute happen, we also say a heart felt thank you. Thanks to Nathan Varley, and Dan MacNulty for their guest appearances at the class.

The Yellowstone Center of Resources, Yellowstone National Park, has been very helpful at all stages, both with their time and constructive comments, especially Norm Bishop, Mike Phillips, and Doug Smith. To these folks -- thank you.

To Joe Vandersnick, our supporter, helper, computer specialist and graphics artist, thank you for all your effort, including late nights.

To anyone that we have inadvertently failed to acknowledge our appreciation, we also say thank you.

To our friends we say, long may the winds blow, the snows fall, and the wolves howl! Let's keep Yellowstone wild.

# TO SEE A WOLF

You are in the right place at the right time! Few people will ever see a free-roaming, wild wolf (*Canis lupus*). Even rarer is the opportunity to hear one howl. Nowhere in the world, has your chance to see wolves ever been as great as in Yellowstone now. You can Increase your chances to see wolves and to understand their behavior. Wolf recovery has provided an unprecedented opportunity to be part of the life of wolves.

Since release in March of 1995, the **Clan of Wolf Watchers**, which includes people like you, have witnessed wolves at play, tending and teaching their young, and other pack behavior. From the side of the road, you may watch the wolf's predatory nature as they chase and kill prey. You may even watch grizzlies and wolves fight over who will eat. Or you may be one of the lucky few to hear the erie low howl of the wolf tumble from the mountain sides.

The year 1996 promises to be even more eventful than was 1995. At least seven packs of wolves may be roaming Yellowstone with dens possibly visible from the roads. Pack social behavior may be observable on nearly a daily basis.

We hope that this booklet will answer questions for this year's **Wolf Watchers**. In addition to introducing the heroes of Yellowstone - **The Wolves**, we hope to help provide a safe and meaningful viewing experience. Inside you will find hints on when, where, and how to see wolves, as well as tips for identifying wolves from their similar appearing cousins, the coyotes. To supplement your viewing experience, we provide a  background about wolves, including an overview of biology, taxonomy, and evolution. We also provide an overview and explanation of the wolf restoration process.

Yellowstone's wolf recovery is far from finished. It is a long road and your wolves will need continued protection. Their future is up to you. Be part of that process, pitch in and help. In the "From Project Leader, Mike Phillips" section, you will find information on how to help the wolves.

# DEDICATION

While there are many heroes in restoring wolves to the West, we should not forget the wolves themselves. It is to those animals that we wish to dedicate this booklet. One wolf stands out above the rest for her role in recovery, **Wolf ~ 9** (see color plates).

**Wolf ~ 9**, we suggest is the Mother Wolf and symbol of wolf recovery to Yellowstone National Park. Her trials and tribulations have been many. She has persevered through translocation from her Canadian home, separation from her original mate, death of her new mate, and natural disaster to her acclimation pen, mothered the largest litter of free-roaming wolves in the Yellowstone Ecosystem, and bore her second litter of pups in Yellowstone National Park in 1996!

During capture, she was separated from her Canadian mate. Brought to Yellowstone in 1995, she was already in mating condition. Despite reservations of how she might react, an new male wolf was placed in her pen. The pairing worked, and they mated. Upon release, she journeyed far to the north with Wolf ~ 10 who was illegally shot and killed. She gave birth to eight pups on the ground. **Wolf ~ 9** moved them to a humble shelter.

**Wolf ~ 9** and her pups faced a bleak future. In unknown country, without other wolves helping, she would have to feed and protect the litter. Additionally, some people in the area did not support restoration creating concern for the wolves' welfare. Pups reared at the edge of the plains might not have dispersed back into the mountains but rather may have stayed in livestock country. Therefore, biologists re-trapped **Wolf ~ 9** and her pups and transported them by helicopter to Rose Creek pen in Yellowstone. Natural disaster struck on July 29, when giant trees were blown onto her pen, crushing the fence but missing **Wolf ~ 9** and her pups. On release, October 12, 1995, she was joined by Wolf ~ 8, and they now lead their pack through the Northern Range of Yellowstone, successfully raising young. She has already outlived one pup born in her "new world," Wolf ~ 22 was hit by a truck.

This spring, after wolves ~ 9 and ~ 8 were observed mating, they localized along Hellroaring Creek in April. On May 3, 1996, three pups were observed at a den site. There may be more, as yet unseen pups. Ask a ranger naturalist or at the information desk for the latest news.

**Wolf ~ 9**, we salute you! May your pups prosper and your genes long flow in the heart of the Yellowstone Ecosystem!

# VIEWING WOLVES

## Safety and Etiquette

Your **safety** in Yellowstone is your responsibility. Protect yourself from people, traffic, and animals such as bison, elk, or bears while viewing. Keep your children under control and away from animals. To observe wolves, use turnouts when possible, even if it means driving to a parking pullout and walking back to view. Lock your car when leaving. Watch for traffic while walking. If a turnout is not available, you may only pull off on established road shoulder. Pull your vehicle completely off the road. Never obstruct traffic. Be especially careful near curves. If animals are close, stay near your car! Do not approach any mammals as these are wild animals and may quickly cause injury if they feel threatened or disturbed. By approaching a carcass or den site, you may displace animals or encounter a grizzly.

**Safety of the animals** is everyone's concern. Your viewing pleasure should never place an animal in danger. Drive slowly when near animals. Whenever possible, view animals from your car, as they are not disturbed as much by cars as they are by people. By approaching or feeding wildlife you may play a part in their eventual removal and destruction. Do not feed, call, or whistle at wildlife. Animals, such as coyotes and ground squirrels, quickly habituate to humans, thus endangering themselves and people. Animals may get hit by cars when too close to the road, and if they begin begging food, they may have to be killed to prevent bites. Never cause an animal to move to where it may become endangered, such as onto a road, into a river, or near a cliff. Intentionally disturbing any wildlife is prohibited by Federal regulations.

**Good viewing etiquette** requires that you not to bother animals. Your presence should not alter an animal's behavior. If animals change their behavior, such as eating or resting, and begin to focus on you, you have approached too closely. Move away immediately. Use binoculars or a spotting scope from a greater distance. Use telephoto lens to photograph animals. Do not attempt to "stimulate" action for pictures; wait for the animal to move. Do not move in front of others taking pictures.

**QUIET, QUIET, QUIET.** Our voices, radios, and motors mask the pristine sounds of wilderness and disturb animals. At viewing sites be especially quiet. Wolves at den sites will be very sensitive to the presence of humans. Respect their silence. Do not howl because your imitation howl may be competitive to territorial wolves, and it is illegal. All opportunity to hear a wolf howl can be destroyed by loud talking, or car motors. When getting out, push car doors quietly, but firmly shut. Turn your car motor off, for silence and to prevent breathing exhaust. Talk softly and listen to nature.

We must **police our own activities**. If others are being loud, endangering wildlife or people, politely ask them to stop. Often unknowing people will quickly change their routines when they understand the impact of their behavior. You may report violations of park rules to rangers.

**Please, keep wolf viewing areas clean, quiet, and safe!**

## The Best Place and Time

While the wolves of Yellowstone have been exceptionally visible since their introduction, there are NEVER any guarantees that you can see them. However, these are tricks-of-the-trade that biologists and dedicated wolf watchers use that improve your chances of seeing wolves.

Most importantly, you have to be in the area when wolves are moving. Wolves may move at any time they get hungry, but they tend to move in the mornings just after daylight and in the evening before sunset. In 1995, 60% of the sightings were between sunrise and 8:00 a.m.; 40% occurred in the evening after 6:00 p.m. If you want to see wolves, be on site by 5:30 to 6:00 in the morning. Do as wolves do. Get up early and nap in the middle of the day. May and June are the best summer months. By July, when it gets hot and the elk go to the high mountains, so will the wolves.

Wolves have been most visible in Lamar Valley. Three packs, Crystal Creek, Leopold, and Rose Creek, use the area from Lava Creek to Soda Butte. In 1995, the hottest area was upstream from the narrows of the Lamar Canyon. This is a good bet for 1996, but try Hellroaring overlook, Slough Creek turnout, and the Blacktail Deer Plateau.

Arrive early. Use binoculars or spotting scopes to scan the lower tree line in the valleys and the open patches on the hillsides. Look under the trees and as deep into the forest as you can. Watch for movement and black animals. The black wolves are easier to spot than are the gray ones. Watch for elk and bison movement. If the elk are very alert and watching one area, or if they move quickly from an area, watch that area carefully. When driving, watch people along the road. If they are intently watching an area stop and see why. If they are simply visiting, drive on.

# WOLVES OF YELLOWSTONE

The last wild Yellowstone wolves were killed in 1926 as part of the "settling of the West," that included a government policy of predator extermination. Under mandates in the Endangered Species Act of 1973, to maintain and restore ecosystems, the U.S. Fish and Wildlife Service and National Park Service brought 31 wolves from Canada to Yellowstone to re-establish the missing population.

The Yellowstone area, comprised of national parks, forests, and wildlife refuges was chosen because it is largely intact and includes many designated wilderness areas. We call the area, the Yellowstone Ecosystem because of its ecological importance and interconnectedness of managing federal and state lands. Wolves are being recovered in the Yellowstone Ecosystem, but for logistical convenience their initial arrival centered on Yellowstone National Park. However, recovery was planned so that wolves would disperse from release sites to the entire ecosystem.

## Acclimation Pens and Release Sites

When the wolves were first translocated to Yellowstone, they were placed in acclimation pens (map inside back cover). The temporary pens were up to one acre in size and held from 2 to 6 wolves. Each pen also contained several security boxes, about 4x4x3 ft in size, where wolves could enter and hide when humans approached for feeding or hide from each other if they were "low dog on the totem pole" within the social dominance hierarchy of the pack. Wolves did not use the boxes for protection from weather but preferred to be outside.

The purpose of the pens was to reduce the homing instinct of the wolves. Previous research suggested that keeping wolves at a new site for an extended period reduces the biological drive to return to their old home.

In 1995, three pen sites were Crystal Creek, Rose Creek, and Soda Butte. In 1996, Crystal and Rose were again used, but the pen at Soda Butte was dismantled. Two new pens, Blacktail and Nez Perce were constructed during the summer of 1996 in preparation for the arrival of new wolves.

By the time the Class of 1996 arrived, wolves had established territories around the Crystal Creek and Blacktail pens. When wolves were placed in the Crystal Creek pen, the Rose Creek Pack centered activities around the newcomers. Park service personnel guarding the wolf pens reported that wolves howled back and forth through the fence and that scuffles actually broke out through the fence as members of Rose Creek and Chief Joseph packs tried to get at each other.

To provide the new wolves areas that were not already occupied by wolves willing to defend their territories, it was decided to transport Lone Star and Chief Joseph packs south. This would help spread wolves over the Park landscape. The Lone Star Pack was taken to near Lone Star Geyser. Because bad weather stopped the movement of the Crystal Creek pen wolves to the southern part of the Park, they were transferred to Nez Perce Pen site for release. Since the Rose Creek pen and the Nez Perce pen were not in existing territories, the pens were simply opened to release the Druid Peak and Nez Perce Packs, respectively.

## Naming Packs and Wolves

Wolf recovery was predicated on establishing **breeding packs** in the ecosystem. The currency of recovery is the breeding pack and its genetic stock. Wolves brought to Yellowstone represent six maternal lines from two geographically separate areas of Canada.

Wolf packs are usually named after a prominent geographic feature within their territory. For Yellowstone, geographic and Native American names have been used. Wolves of the **Class of 1995** comprise four packs: Crystal Creek, Leopold, Rose Creek, and Soda Butte. Wolves from the **Class of 1996** comprised four packs on release: Chief Joseph, Druid Peak, Lone Star, and Nez Perce.

One exception to name guidelines has been to honor Aldo Leopold. In 1944, Leopold championed returning wolves to Yellowstone, even while they were being destroyed elsewhere. The Leopold pack is the first pack to form in the wild and, hopefully, produce pups.

Early on in the Yellowstone recovery process, a decision was made not to name individual wolves as a sign of our respect. Wolves certainly would not choose names for their young that humans might. Would wolves call themselves, blacky or fang? Might they instead chose Swift Chaser of Fleet Elk or something more appropriate?. Therefore, out of respect, the wolves of Yellowstone will be known by pseudonyms - numbers, which we know is not what they call themselves.

**The secret of their names will remain with the wolves.**

# GETTING TO KNOW YOUR WOLVES

The **year book** of Yellowstone wolves is your quick guide to packs and their members. It is a **portrait in time**, at the beginning of **May 1995**, and there may well be changes by the time you purchase your watcher's guide. To remain updated when you leave Yellowstone, we suggest you purchase a **pack sponsorship kit** available in the park or from Call of the Wild Foundation (see Learning About Wolves).

The year book includes portraits, biographies, family trees, location maps, pack composition diagrams, and a quick visual key to pack and individual wolf identification. Portraits, quick key, and location maps are in the color plate section. Wolves are grouped by arrival period as the Class of 1995 and 1996.

**Individual biographies** are provided for ardent Wolf Watchers. Biographies explain what we know about the life of different wolves and provides clues for identifying wolves in the field. Some wolves, are not too well known, partly because many of the pups look similar and the Class of 1996 has not roamed free long enough to establish their reputations. When available we have included class portraits.

Hair color and patterns are major clues to visual identification. Hair color will change seasonally, with each new molt, and with different lighting. Toward the end of the winter, the hair becomes sun bleached, and after the spring and fall molting, hair color is bright. Coat color becomes lighter with age. To aid in identification, look for patterns of light and dark hair and distinctive markings. Compare to other wolves near by.

**Location maps** are also matriarchical. For the Class of 1995, the outer, lighter-colored area represents the range explored by the female, her geographic and historical knowledge range. The inner, darker-colored area represents the approximate territory used during the winter of 1995-96. For the Class of 1996, the area shown approximates the April and May explorations by the recently released wolves.

**Family trees** show our knowledge, though incomplete, of genetic relatedness of wolves brought to Yellowstone. Genetic studies are needed to answer questions about some relationships.

Family tree diagrams are matriarchical and, if known, show by number female matings to males. For example, female Wolf~9 has had three male mates: one in Canada, Wolf~10, and Wolf~8. Wolves are indicated by a number followed by F for female or M for male. Arrows point to young born to a pair. Color, age, and weight are shown below the animal. Age and weight were taken when animals were handled either at capture in Canada or as pups in the acclimation pen. Birth and death dates (known or estimated) are also listed.

**Pack composition diagrams** show the history of established packs and lone wolves. Since wolves may leave one pack and form or join another pack, composition diagrams differ from family trees. Significant events and dates are shown in the history of packs. Diagrams are read from left to right and track the history of each member.

**The quick visual key** provides for easy reference pack composition and some family tree history. It allows you to see how many animals and who should be present in a pack. However, at any given time some animals may be on their own. The key shows general color, black or grey, alpha animals, and age distribution. Deceased wolves are indicated by a red "X" and transfers between packs by blue arrow. The quick key represents a **point in time around the beginning of May 1996**.

# Class of 1995

Wolves of the Class of 1995 were translocated from near Hinton, Alberta, Canada in two shipments arriving in Yellowstone on January 12 and 19, 1995. The first shipment included the Crystal Creek Pack of six and wolves ~7 and ~9 from the Rose Creek Pack. The second shipment included wolf ~10 and the Soda Butte Pack of five, bringing the total to 14. Two packs reproduced, Soda and Crystal, with one and eight pups respectively. Five wolves died in various manners (~3, ~10, ~11, ~12, and ~22). Eighteen wolves from the class of 1995 now roam free in the ecosystem. At least three pups were born to Wolf ~9 before press time.

## Crystal Creek Pack

Upon release the Crystal Creek Pack spent most of its time in Lamar Valley. When the spring snow hardened enough to easily support wolves, the Crystal Pack explored northeast out of the Park over the Beartooth mountains almost to Red Lodge, Montana. The short exploration trip lasted about a week, and since then Crystal has spent most of its time in Lamar and Pelican Valleys. In 1996, they denned near the Soda Butte geothermal formation.

**Wolf ~5** is the alpha female of Crystal. She was observed digging five dens during May of 1995. Although biologists assumed she was pregnant, Wolf ~ 5 did not produce a litter. Evidently, Wolf ~ 5 went through a pseudopregnancy. Although her hormones told her to prepare a den, no young were born.

*Description: Wolf ~ 5, a gray female, weighed 98 lbs upon arrival from Canada. When traveling with her mate, Wolf ~ 4, she often stays just behind him.*

**Wolf ~ 4** is the alpha male of Crystal. Early in 1995, wolves ~ 4 and ~ 5 led charges on elk. Once, we watched wolves ~ 4 and ~ 5 approach a herd of bison only to be set running as the bison turned on the wolves. By November, wolves ~ 4 and ~ 5 were letting the pups lead and make kills. Then they would take over the kill, exerting their dominance, and feed first.

*Description: Wolf ~ 4, a black male, weighed 98 lbs when brought to the Y.N.P. He can be recognized by his white chest and chin patches.*

**Wolf ~ 6** has remained with his parents since arrival and through the winter of 1996.

*Description: Wolf ~ 6, a brownish-black, male pup weighed 75 lbs on arrival. He can be differentiated from litter mates by his white chest patch. At a distance, he appears as a slightly lighter black.*

**Wolf ~ 3** is deceased (see In Memorial section).
**Wolf ~ 2** is now a member of the Leopold Pack.
**Wolf ~ 8** is now a member of the Rose Creek Pack.

## Leopold Pack

The Leopold Pack, the first free-roaming pack to form in Yellowstone, is comprised of wolves ~ 2 and ~ 7. These two young adults have become alpha members of their own pack. In most wild situations, two-year old animals would not have this opportunity.

**Wolf ~ 7**, has proven to be independent and resourceful. Last seen with her mother on April 3, 1995, she traveled alone during summer and fall. Wolf ~ 7 is known to have killed at least two adult elk by herself. Although she never took a long exploratory trip of her own, her known range has gradually expanded, until 7 knew a large part of the northern range of Yellowstone. She has even ventured near Mammoth and Gardiner. On January 25, 1996, Wolf ~ 7 was traveling with Wolf ~ 2 and they have been together ever since. Together, they now form the Leopold pack. In 1996, they denned on Blacktail Deer Plateau.

*Description: Wolf ~ 7, a young adult gray female, weighed 77 lbs on arrival. She is distinguished by some red hair and up close she appears to slightly reddish-gray.*

**Wolf ~ 2** was last observed with the pack on December 23, 1995. He roamed by himself for awhile before joining **Wolf ~ 7** on January 26, 1996. Together they have settled in the area around Blacktail Plateau. In February 1996, 2 and 7 were observed making double scent marks (urinating together), a sign that they consider their area a territory and that they have probably bred.

*Description: Wolf ~ 2, a black, male young adult, weighed 77 lbs upon arrival. His black color sprinkled with gray quickly differentiates him from his reddish gray mate Wolf ~ 7. He has a light white chest patch.*

## Rose Creek Pack

There have been two reincarnations of the Rose Creek Pack since it was brought to Yellowstone. Female ~ 9 and her pup, Wolf ~ 7 were initially penned with male ~ 10 in the pen upon arrival from Canada. When released, Wolf ~ 7 stayed with her mom for a short while and then ceased to travel with the new pair. When the snow hardened up, Wolves ~ 9 and ~ 10 explored over the Beartooth Plateau to an area within four miles of Red Lodge, MT. A Red Lodge man shot and killed Wolf ~ 10. Wolf ~ 9 then had 8 pups which, with their mother, were later transferred back into the acclimation pen. October 11, when released from the pen, the second Rose Creek pack formed as Wolf ~ 8 joined Wolf ~ 9. In 1996, they denned near the confluence of the Yellowstone River and Hellroaring Creek. Three pups were observed outside the den on May 3, 1996.

**Wolf ~ 9**, the alpha female, was separated from her original mate when brought from Canada. Her resulting history has been detailed in the dedication on page 2.

*Description: Wolf ~ 9, a black adult female, weighed 98 lbs on arrival. There is considerable gray sprinkled in her coat, especially around the face. Her mate, Wolf ~ 8, is gray.*

**Wolf ~ 8**, a pup when brought from Canada, spent most of the summer of 1995 traveling with his parents, but his excursions away from the pack became longer and longer. On his own, he discovered **female ~ 9** and her pups in the Rose Creek acclimation pen. He started visiting them. Two pups locked outside the pen were observed begging food from him on October 11, 1995. When Wolf ~ 9 and her pups were released, they were quickly joined by Wolf ~ 8, who became the third mate of Wolf ~ 9. Together Wolf ~ 8 and Wolf ~ 9 now lead the Rose Creek pack.

*Description: Wolf ~ 8, a gray male young adult, weighed 72 lbs on arrival. His gray color separates him from his blackish-gray mate Wolf ~ 9.*

**Wolf ~ 17** was born in the Rock Creek drainage of the Yellowstone River, near Red Lodge about April 27, 1996. When with the rest of the pups, she is very playful and perhaps even picked on by her litter mates. *Description:* Wolf ~ 17, a gray female yearling, weighed 55 lbs when radio collared in the Rose Creek pen on October 9, 1995. Since there are only two gray wolves, Wolf ~ 8 and Wolf ~ 17, in the pack, she is easily told from her gray adopted father by her distinctly smaller size.

**Wolves ~ 16, ~ 18, and ~ 19**, females, were born in the Rock Creek drainage of the Yellowstone River, near Red Lodge about April 27, 1996.
*Description:* All three female yearlings are black and difficult to tell from litter mates. The weights of 16 and 19 were 57 and 55 lbs. Wolf ~ 18 was free roaming when her litter mates were released so she has been neither weighed nor collared.

**Wolves ~ 20, ~ 21, and ~ 23**, males, were born in the Rock Creek drainage of the Yellowstone River, near Red Lodge about April 27, 1996.
*Description:* All three male yearlings are black and difficult to tell from litter mates. Wolf ~ 20 was slightly smaller at 55 lbs on October 9, 1995 than his mates are 57 lbs. Wolf ~ 23 was free roaming when the rest were released and therefore is not radio collared.

**Wolf ~ 10** is deceased (see In Memorial section).

**Wolf ~ 22** is deceased (see In Memorial section).

## Soda Butte Pack

Soda Butte pack has spent most of its time north of the park. They too showed initial post-release movements near their pen, and hunted the waters of Soda Butte Creek, but soon took an exploratory trip over the Beartooths to the Stillwater River. Most of their time has been spent in the Stillwater drainage, where they denned. There female ~ 14 gave birth, but only one pup was ever observed. If more than one was born, the others perished early in life. This would not be unexpected because pup mortality can be high early in life. In 1996, they denned on the Rosebud Creek near Roscoe, Montana. Although observed near cattle, the pack has not harassed any domestic stock.

**Wolf ~ 13** is the alpha male of the pack. His worn teeth indicate great age and "wisdom". Blue, as 13 has been called is very timid. When biologists approached the pen to feed, Blue always ran to his security box and hid. Initially, he was seldom seen by ground observers, keeping to the trees. He became known to some as the gray ghost. The possibility exists that Wolf ~ 13 fathered the rest of this pack.

*Description: Wolf ~ 13, an adult male, weighed 113 lbs on arrival. Wolf ~ 13 is unusual in that his coated color is blue, as blue as the Arctic fox and glacier blue bears of Alaska. The blue, or gun-metal gray, color derives from long grayish hairs intermingled with darker black hairs which together glint as a bluish color.*

**Wolf ~ 14**, the alpha female of the pack was a young adult on arrival from Canada. She did not show signs of having previously bred.

*Description: Wolf ~ 14, a young adult female, weighed 89 lbs on arrival. Wolf ~ 14 is gray with very light fur on top of her tail separating her black tip from the body.*

**Wolf ~ 15** was a young adult upon arrival from Canada.

*Description: Wolf ~ 15, a black young adult male, was not weighed when brought to Yellowstone. Wolf ~ 15 has a light brown patch, called a saddle, which is often visible over his shoulders. Sometimes the patch is very prominent.*

**Wolf ~ 24** was born in the Yellowstone Ecosystem along the Stillwater River about the end of April, 1995. Since Wolf ~ 24 has never been handled, we do not know its sex, but suspect it is a male based on behavior observed during radio tracking flights. The pack initially stayed near the Stillwater, but by fall was beginning to travel and Wolf ~ 24 was often absent from the pack for extended periods of time. Presumably, Wolf ~ 24 stayed in the Stillwater drainage, but since Wolf ~ 24 has not been collared, its location is often not known. During the spring of 1996, Wolf ~ 24 was again traveling with the pack.

*Description: Wolf ~ 24 is a black wolf. Wolf ~ 24 has mostly been observed during aerial flights and its distinctive markings have yet to be described.*

**Wolf ~ 11** *is deceased (see In Memorial section).*
**Wolf ~ 12** *is deceased (see In Memorial section).*

# *Family Trees for Yellowstone Wolves*
## Class of 1995

### *Crystal Creek*

| | | | | |
|---|---|---|---|---|
| **Unknown** | previous mate | **4 M**<br>(Black, Alpha, 98) | --> | **2 M**<br>(Black, Pup, 77) |
| | | | --> | **3 M**<br>(Black, Pup, 80, 2/5/96) |
| | | | --> | **6 M**<br>(Black, Pup, 75) |
| | | | --> | **8 M**<br>(Gray, Pup, 72) |
| **5 F**<br>(Gray, Alpha, 98) | +1) 1/12/95 | | | |

### *Rose Creek*

| | | | | |
|---|---|---|---|---|
| **9 F**<br>(Black, Alpha, 98) | +1) previous mate | **Unknown** | ---> | **7 F**<br>(Gray, Pup, 77) |
| | +2) 1/19/95 | **10 M**<br>(Gray, Alpha, 122, 4/26/96) | --> | **16 F**<br>(4/27/95, Black, PUP, 57) |
| | | | --> | **17F**<br>(4/27/95, Gray, PUP, 55) |
| | | | --> | **18F**<br>(4/27/95, Black, PUP, no weight) |
| | | | --> | **19F**<br>(4/27/95, Black, PUP, 55) |
| | | | --> | **20M**<br>(4/27/95, Black, PUP, 55) |
| | | | --> | **21M**<br>(4/27/95, Black, PUP, 57) |
| | | | --> | **22M**<br>(4/27/95, Black, PUP, 57, 12/19/95) |
| | | | --> | **23M**<br>(4/27/95, Black, PUP, 57) |
| | +3) 10/11/95 | **8M**<br>(Gray, Alpha) | ---> | Pups born<br>(mid-April/96) |

### *Soda Butte*

| | | | | |
|---|---|---|---|---|
| **14F**<br>(Gray, Alpha, 89) | +1) 1/19/95 | **13M**<br>(Blue, Alpha, 113) | ---> | **24?M**<br>(4/95, Black) |
| **11F**<br>(Gray, AD, 92, 3/30/96) | | Relationships within the Soda Butte pack are not known.,<br>Wolf~13M may have fathered Wolves~11F, ~12M, ~14 F and ~15M. | | |
| **12M**<br>(Black, AD, 122, 2/11/96) | | Neither female~11 nor ~14 had produced young before capture. | | |
| **15M**<br>(Black, SA) | | Genetic evidence of relationships is needed and<br>could be obtained from existing blood samples. | | |

Ages are for wolves at time of arrival to Yellowstone.
Weights are at time of arrival or when pups were being prepared for release from Rose Creek pen.
Date at left end of parentheses is date of birth, that at right is date of death.

# Pack Composition
## Class of 1995

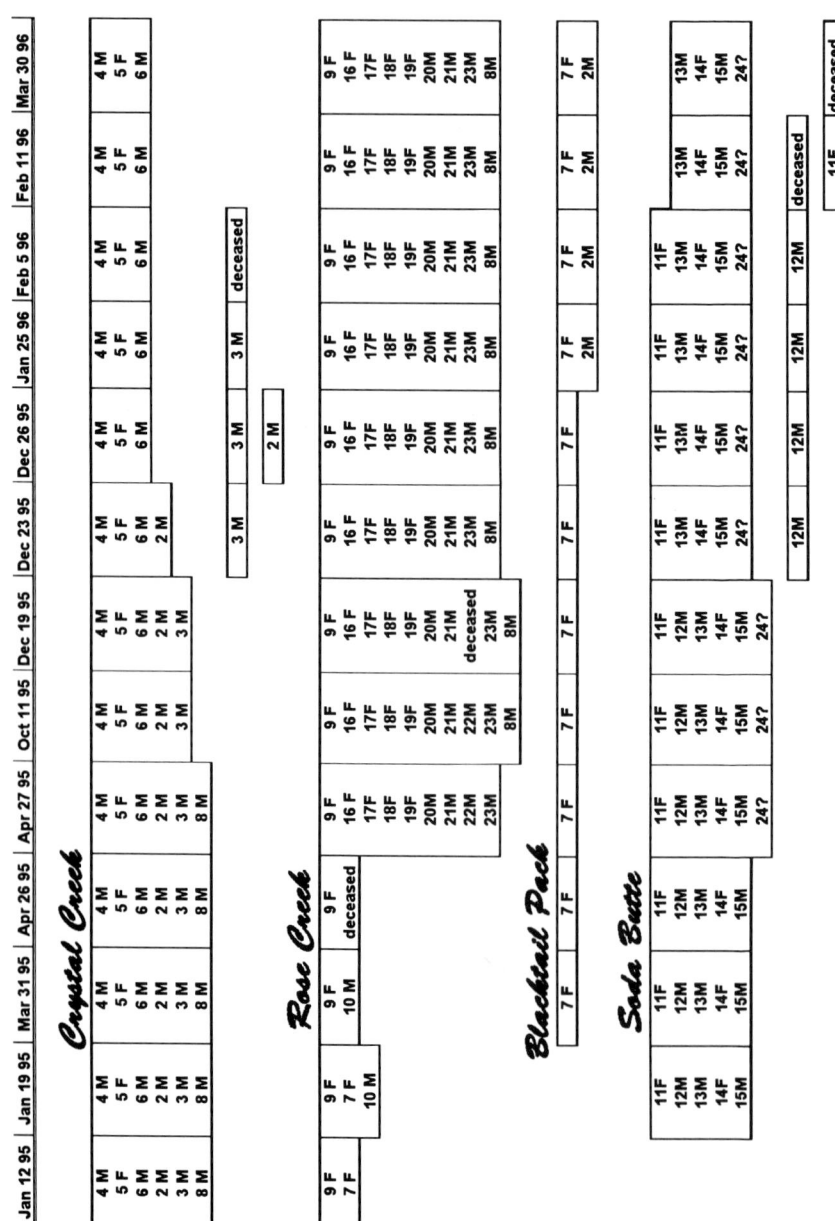

Halfpenny and Thompson -- 14

# Class of 1996

Wolves of the Class of 1996 were translocated from near Fort St. John, British Columbia (page 50), Canada. Two shipments arrived in Yellowstone on January 23 and 27, 1996. The first shipment included 11 wolves of the Lone Star, Chief Joseph, and Nez Perce Packs. The second shipment included six wolves of the Druid Peak Pack and Wolf ~ 37 who was re-joined with her pack, the Nez Perce Pack. Wolves from the Class of 1996 were heavier on the average than those of the Class of 1995. Less is known about members of the Class of 1996 as they have not had time to establish reputations yet.

## Chief Joseph Pack

The Chief Joseph Pack was formed in Yellowstone by pairing wolves from two different packs from Canada: wolves ~ 31, ~ 32, ~ 33 with wolf ~ 34. The Chief Joseph Pack resided in Crystal Creek acclimation pen. and were transported to the Nez Perce pen on April 11, 1996. Wolves ~ 32, 33, and 34 have traveled together west and south of the pen to Old Faithful. From there they wandered north of West Yellowstone along Hebgen and Earthquake Lakes. At press time, the pack was in Paradise Valley not far from Emigrant, Montana and had not denned.

**Wolf ~ 32** is the currently the alpha female. Lack of tooth wear suggests that she is a young adult. She showed no signs of having bred.

*Description: Wolf ~ 32, a gray adult female, weighed 90 lbs on arrival.*

**Wolf ~ 34** is the alpha male. His small size also suggests that he may have been a young adult.

*Description: Wolf ~ 34, a gray adult male, weighed 106 lbs on arrival.*

**Wolf ~ 31** was a pup on arrival from Canada. His parents are not known. Wolf ~ 34 is not his mother, but may be an older sister.

*Description: Wolf ~ 31, a gray male yearling, weighed 96 lbs on arrival. He has a very grizzled appearing face and distinct white saddle over his shoulders.*

**Wolf ~ 33** was a pup on arrival from Canada. Her Parents are not known. Wolf ~ 34 is not her mother, but may be an older sister.

*Description: Wolf ~ 33, a black female yearling, weighed 96 lbs on arrival.*

## Druid Peak Pack

The Druid Peak Pack was formed in Yellowstone by pairing wolves from two different packs from Canada: wolves ~39, ~40, ~41, and ~42 with male ~38. They resided in Rose Creek acclimation pen. On April 2, 1996 biologists removed a panel from the acclimation pen. The Druid pack remained in the pen for 12 days. then they explored up Slough Creek to the headwaters of the Stillwater River, over to Wolverine Creek and then to Lake Abundance Creek. Since they spent considerable time in Wolverine Creek drainage, there was speculation that they may have denned. However, just before press time they moved southeast of Cooke City.

**Wolf ~39** is the alpha female and she brought her three pups with her. Her Canadian mate is unknown.

*Description: Wolf ~39, a gray adult female, weighed 93 lbs on arrival. Wolf ~39 is so light in color that she appears almost white at a distance.*

**Wolf ~38** is the alpha male.

*Description: Wolf ~38, a gray adult male, weighed 115 lbs on arrival.*

**Wolf ~40** was born in Canada and is a pup of Wolf ~39.

*Description: Wolf ~40, a gray female yearling, weighed 94 lbs on arrival.*

**Wolves ~41, and ~42**, born in Canada, are yearlings of Wolf ~39.

*Description: Wolves ~41 and ~42, black, female pups, weighed 80 and 92 lbs respectively on arrival.*

## Lone Star Pack

The Lone Star Pack was formed in Yellowstone by pairing wolves from two different packs from Canada: female ~36 and male ~35 They resided in Blacktail acclimation pen until their release north of Lone Star Geyser. They explored around the release site to a couple of miles south of Lone Star Geyser. Wolf ~36 was discovered dead on April 14, 1966. On April 15, her mate, Wolf ~35, was observed 14 mi south of the release site. He has not be located since then, but there have been rumors of a wolf west of Grand Teton National Park. The loss of female ~36 effectively terminates this pack after only nine days in the wild.

**Wolf ~35** was the alpha male.

*Description: Wolf ~35, a black adult male, weighed 120 lbs on arrival.*

**Wolf ~36** is deceased (see In Memorial section).

# Nez Perce Pack

The Nez Perce Pack, which consists of all member of one pack in Canada, arrived in two shipments from Canada, but all wolves are original members of the pack in Canada. This pack was captured while feeding on a bison carcass in Canada. They were placed in the Nez Perce acclimation pen. Members of the Nez Perce Pack did not stay together when the pen was open. The females left the pen immediately while the males stay in the pen for 2 more days. Together the females headed northeast covering 30 miles the first day. They quickly reached the east edge of the park and traveled past Cooke City to Clay Butte along the Clark's Fork to south of Red Lodge, Montana. Wolf ~ 27 left her pups and traveled north to I-90 near Reedpoint but returned to near Red Lodge and has now localized near the Stillwater River. This may indicate that she is pregnant. Yearlings ~ 26 and ~ 30 localized east and south of Red Lodge. Yearling ~ 37 has been alone near Red Lodge, but just moved to near Wolf ~ 27. The males initially traveled east to Canyon in the Park, then northwest past Mt. Everts, and Tower to the Paradise Valley. In Late April, they were traveling separately up and down the Paradise Valley to north of Emigrant, Montana. In 1996, female ~ 27 denned south of Nye, Montana.

**Wolf ~ 27** is the alpha female and she was accompanied by her mate, 28, from Canada..

*Description: Wolf ~ 27, a gray adult female weighed 115 lbs on arrival.*

**Wolf ~ 28**, the alpha male accompanied his mate, Wolf ~ 28, from Canada.

*Description: Wolf ~ 28, a gray adult male weighed 130 lbs on arrival. He was 8 lbs heavier than any other wolf brought to Yellowstone and biologist's said simply "a massive wolf."*

**Wolves ~ 26, ~ 30, and ~ 37** are yearlings born in Canada to Wolves ~ 27 and ~ 28.

*Description: Wolves ~ 26, ~ 30, and ~ 37 are gray, female yearlings. Wolf ~ 30 weighed 100 lbs and 37 weighed 90 lbs on arrival. No weight was available for 26.*

**Wolf ~ 29** is a pup born in Canada to ~ 27 and ~ 28.

*Description: Wolf ~ 30, a gray, male yearling weighed 100 lbs on arrival.*

# Family Trees for Yellowstone Wolves
## Class of 1996

### Lone Star Pack
Blacktail Acclimation Pen

| 36 F<br>(Black, Alpha, 103, 4/14/96) | +1) 1/23/96 | 35 M<br>(Black, Alpha, 120) |
|---|---|---|

### Chief Joseph Pack
Crystal Creek Acclimation Pen

| 32 F (Gray, Alpha, 90)<br>31 M (Gray, Pup, 96)<br>33 F (Black, Pup, 96) | +1) 1/23/96 | 34 M (Gray, Alpha, 106)<br>Wolf~32 had never bred and is not the mother of ~31 and ~33 |
|---|---|---|

### Druid Peak Pack
Rose Creek Acclimation Pen

| 39 F<br>(Gray, Alpha, 93) | +1) previous mate | **Unknown** | --> 40 F (Gray, Pup, 94)<br>--> 41 F (Black, Pup, 80)<br>--> 42 F (Black, Pup, 92) |
|---|---|---|---|
|  | +2) 1/27/96 | 38 M (Gray, AD, 115) |  |

### Nez Perce
Nez Perce Acclimation Pen

| 27 F<br>(Gray, Alpha, 115) | +1) original mates | 28 M<br>(Gray, Alpha, 130) | --> 26 F (Gray, Pup, no weight)<br>--> 29 M (Gray, Pup, 100)<br>--> 30 F (Gray, Pup, 100)<br>--> 37 F (Gray, Pup, 90) |
|---|---|---|---|

Ages are for wolves at time of arrival to Yellowstone.
Weights were taken in Canada before shipment to Yellowstone.
Date at right end of parentheses is date of death.

# Pack Composition
## Class of 1996

| Jan 23, 1996 | Jan 27, 1996 | Apr 14, 199 |

### Lone Star
Blacktail Acclimation Pen

| | | |
|---|---|---|
| 35 M | 35 M | 35 M |
| 36 F | 36 F | deceased |

### Chief Joseph
Crystal Creek Acclimation Pen

| | | |
|---|---|---|
| 31 M | 31 M | 31 M |
| 32 F | 32 F | 32 F |
| 33 F | 33 F | 33 F |
| 34 M | 34 M | 34 M |

### Druid Peak
Rose Creek Acclimation Pen

| | | |
|---|---|---|
| | 38 M | 38 M |
| | 39 F | 39 F |
| | 40 F | 40 F |
| | 41 F | 41 F |
| | 42 F | 42 F |

### Nez Perce
Nez Perce Acclimation Pen

| | | |
|---|---|---|
| 26 F | 26 F | 26 F |
| 27 F | 27 F | 27 F |
| 28 M | 28 M | 28 M |
| 29 M | 29 M | 29 M |
| 30 F | 30 F | 30 F |
| | 37 F | 37 F |

# In Memorial

Sixteen months after the first translocation, six wolves have died. Their deaths have varied from natural accident to human-caused accident to deliberate murder. However, the amount of mortality has been relatively low compared to levels sustained in free-living populations. Survivorship has far exceeded original hopes for the project, and wolves are well on the way to recovery. It is an honor to those that have perished to know that 34 wolves still roam the Yellowstone Ecosystem and that there may be as many as seven litters this spring.

Those that have died are listed by pack below.

## Crystal Creek Pack:

**Wolf ~ 3** was last observed with the pack on December 21, 1995. He traveled by himself for a while, finally heading north along the Yellowstone River into Paradise Valley. There Wolf ~ 3, killed two sheep. Animal Damage Control personnel live-trapped Wolf ~ 3 and translocated him to the rose creek pen and then to Pelican Valley in the Park. Within 9 days, he had returned to Paradise Valley and was again harassing sheep. According to operating procedures established by the wolf recovery plan, Wolf ~ 3 had used up his two chances and had to be removed from the ecosystem. While Wolf ~ 3 technically could have been live trapped and moved, the expediency of meeting wolf recovery obligations to agricultural concerns necessitated shooting Wolf ~ 3 for a quick removal.

*Description: Wolf ~ 3, a black, male yearling at his time of death, weighed 80 lbs on arrival.*

## Rose Creek Pack:

**Wolf ~ 10** was one of the two largest wolves brought from Canada in 1995. He was bold; when other wolves retreated to the back of the pens during feeding, Wolf ~ 10 would watch the biologists directly. As soon as they left, he would approach and investigate the offered meat. A fitting tribute to Wolf ~ 10 is the legacy of 8 pups that he sired before his untimely death.

*Description: Wolf ~ 10, a gray male adult, weighed 122 lbs on arrival. His portrait with its clearly black-tipped ears graces a poster for sale in the park to help support the wolf project.*

**Wolf ~ 22** was born in the Rock Creek drainage of the Yellowstone River, near Red Lodge about April 27, 1996. He was killed by a UPS truck on the night of December 19, 1995 as he crossed the road in Lamar Canyon.
*Description: Wolf ~ 22, a black male pup, who weighed 57 lbs on October 9, 1996.*

### Soda Butte Pack:
**Wolf ~ 11** was a young adult on arrival from Canada. She did not show signs of having previously bred. Wolf ~ 11, was last seen with the pack on February 10, 1996. After roaming alone, she was shot and killed on March 30, 1996 near Meeteetse, Wyoming.
*Description: Wolf ~ 11 was a dark gray wolf, who weighed 92 lbs on arrival. The top of her tail was dark to the tip.*

**Wolf ~ 12** was a young adult upon arrival from Canada. Wolf ~ 12 tied for the second heaviest wolf of the Class of 1996 at 122 lbs. Many thought he would be the alpha male of the pack, but speculations were dashed when, after December 21, 1995, Wolf ~ 12 was no longer observed with the pack. He dispersed south over the Absaroka mountain range to near Dubois, Wyoming. Perhaps his journey then took him farther south over the Wind River Range. Whatever his route, he was found dead on February 11, 1996 southeast from Jackson, Wyoming along a snowmobile trail. Wolf ~ 12 had been shot and killed. A reward has been posted for information as to the killer of Wolf ~ 12.
*Description: Numbers 12, a black adult male, weighed 122 lbs on arrival.*

### Lone Star Pack
**Wolf ~ 36** became the alpha female on arrival in Yellowstone. On April 14, 1996 her radio collar gave a mortality signal. The mortality signal tells biologists that the wolf has not moved for six hours. On April 15, biologists went to the signal and found Wolf ~ 36 dead. Examination showed that she had died from thermal burns. Since Wolf ~ 36 was not familiar with hot water she may have accidently entered a pool. Wolf ~ 36 was pregnant with four male and two female pups at the time of her death, making this an especially tragic event.
*Description: Wolf ~ 36, a black adult female, weighed 103 lbs on arrival.*

# HOW TO IDENTIFY A WOLF

## Wolves

The handling of the large number of wolves trapped for translocation provided a unique opportunity for scientists to learn about wild wolves. Besides general health, each wolf was checked for diseases including rabies, tuberculosis, brucellosis, parvo virus, and canine distemper. Sex, age, and color were determined for each wolf. These data provide a clear picture of the wolves inhabiting Yellowstone.

## Weights and Growth

The distribution of **weights of translocated wolves** is shown below. Each weighed wolf is shown by sex as an individual bar, the length of which equals the weight. In 1995, females averaged 91 lbs and males averaged 95 lbs. The largest female was 98 lbs and the largest male 122 lbs. The wolves brought in 1996 were larger; females averaged 93 lbs and males averaged 109 lbs. The largest female in 1996 was 115 lbs and the largest male 130 lbs.

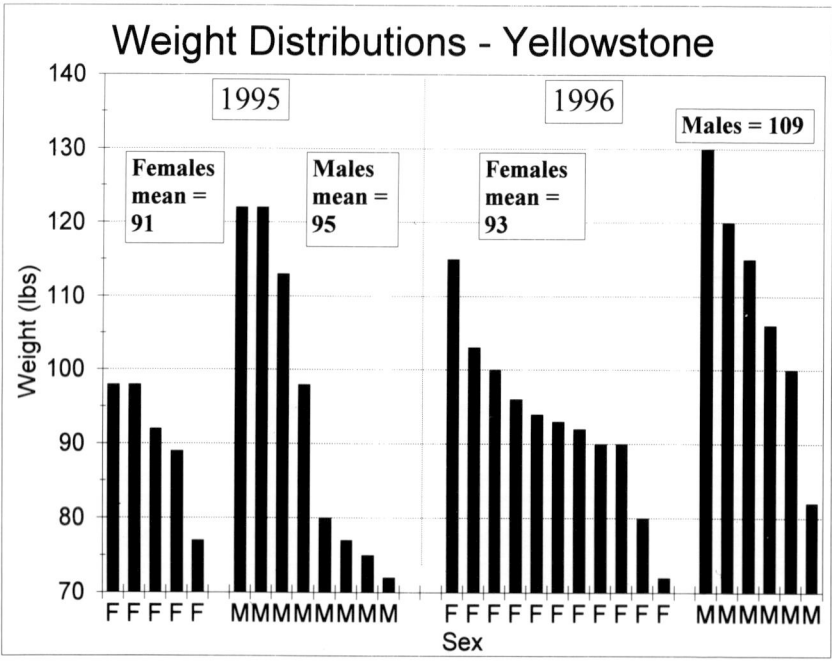

Weights of wolves translocated to Yellowstone National Park categorized by year and by sex (F= female, M = male).

By graphing weights against the estimated ages of captured wolves, it is possible to obtain a crude estimate of growth rates. The two lines on the graph provide approximate growth curves for female (lower line) and male (upper line) wolves. Males grow faster and reach heavier weights than do females. To use the graph, select an age and draw an imaginary line perpendicular to the x-axis up to the line for the sex wolf you wish to know about. Next draw an imaginary line horizontally to the left until it intersects the y-axis and estimate the weight.

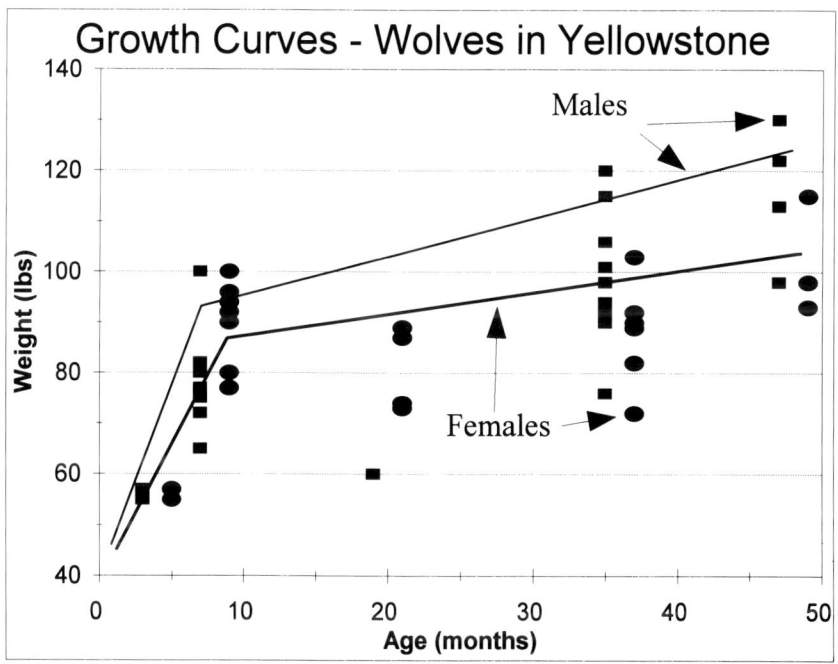

Approximate growth curves for male and female wolves translocated to Yellowstone.

## Wolf Colors

Most wolves (56%) captured in Canada were gray, with the distinctive reddish-gray color of Wolf ~ 7 and bluish-gray color of Wolf ~ 13 rarely occurring (1%). Equal numbers of black and gray wolves were brought to Yellowstone in 1995, but seven more gray than black wolves were brought in 1996 bringing the total to 61% gray for translocated wolves. Black colored wolves are easy to separate from coyotes, but not the majority of the wolves which are gray.

Color distribution of wolves trapped in Canada and of those brought to Yellowstone. Actual numbers are shown in parentheses.

|            | Black     | Gray      | Red/Gray | Blue/Gray |
|------------|-----------|-----------|----------|-----------|
| Canada     | 42% (33)  | 56% (44)  | 1% (1)   | 1% (1)    |
| Yellowstone| 39% (12)  | 55% (17)  | 3% (1)   | 3% (1)    |

## Age and Sex Distribution

Currently, there are 18 females, 15 males, and one suspected male yearling. Seventeen of the wolves are adults and 17 yearlings. With age and sex ratios nearly equal, the potential for additional packs to develop is high. Look for yearlings to disperse during the fall of 1996 and hopefully the new year will usher in new packs.

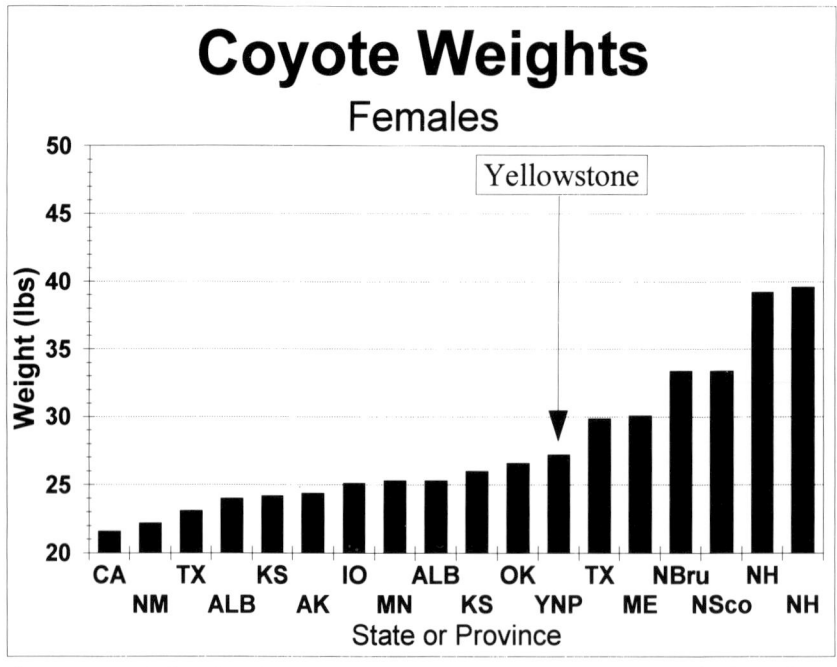

Average weights for female coyote from 18 studies in North America

## Coyotes

The largest male coyote (*Canis latrans*) ever weighed in Yellowstone was 38.5 lbs and the largest female 37.5 lbs. However, the average adult male coyote weighs 33 lbs and the average adult female weighs 27 lbs. While Yellowstone coyotes are a bit above average in size for North America, they are not large. The graph show average weight from 18 studies where coyotes were actually weighed -- no old hunter's tales. The largest coyotes grow in the northeast North America.

## Telling Yellowstone's Canines Apart

At a distance, it can be difficult to tell coyotes from wolves. Experts know this and will spend considerable time studying an unknown canine at a distance with good binoculars or a spotting scope. Remember, experts quickly admit uncertainty, but novices are always sure. The good natural history detective always gathers all the clues possible before making an educated deduction as to identity.

Size is a good clue. Wolves are substantially larger than coyotes, as seen by comparing their weights. The largest coyotes are less than 40 lbs whereas any free roaming wolves are larger than 45 lbs. By the time wolf pups leave the rendezvous site each summer, they usually weigh over 50 lbs. However, body size alone may not be the best characteristic to use in identifying canines unless they are near each other.

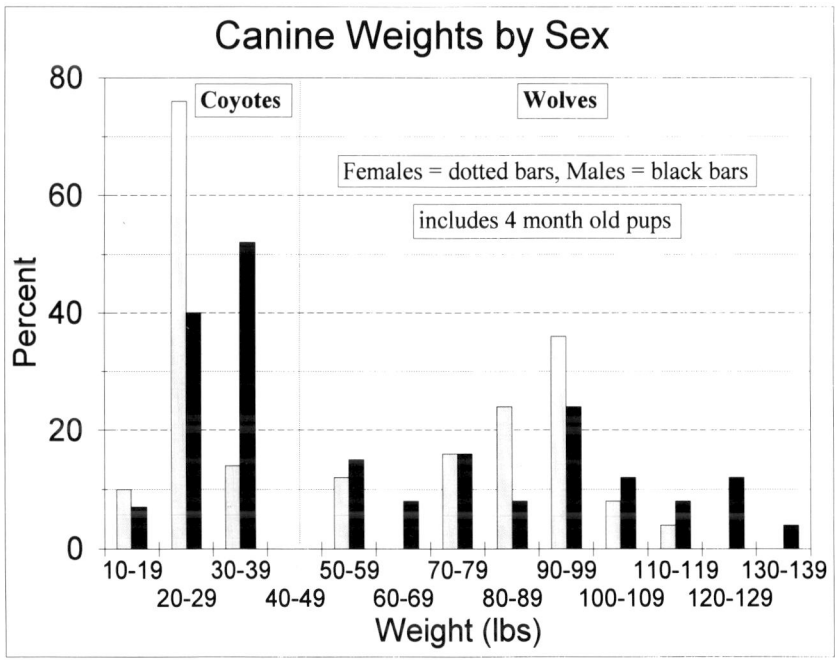

Weights of coyotes and wolves in Yellowstone by sex.

# COLOR PHOTOGRAPHS

# TABLE OF CONTENTS

Saga of Wolf ~ 9 . . . . . . . . . . . . . . . . **1**
Quick Identification Chart . . . . . . . . . . . . **2**
    Class of 1995 . . . . . . . . . . . . . . . . . 2
    Class of 1996 . . . . . . . . . . . . . . . . . 3
Year Book: **Class of 1995** . . . . . . . . . . **4**
    Crystal Creek Pack . . . . . . . . . . . . . . . 4
    Leopold Pack . . . . . . . . . . . . . . . . . . 5
    Rose Creek Pack . . . . . . . . . . . . . . . 6
    Soda Butte Pack . . . . . . . . . . . . . . . . 7
Crystal Alpha Pair Cuts One Out . . . . . . . **8**
Year Book: **Class of 1996** . . . . . . . . . . **10**
    Chief Joseph Pack . . . . . . . . . . . . . . 10
    Druid Peak Pack . . . . . . . . . . . . . . . 11
    Lone Star Pack . . . . . . . . . . . . . . . . 12
    Nez Perce Pack . . . . . . . . . . . . . . . . 13
People and Events . . . . . . . . . . . . . . **14**
Views from the Field . . . . . . . . . . . . . **16**

Additional Color Pages
    Front Cover: Number 10
    Outside Back Cover: Carrying in the first wolf
    Inside Back Cover: Pens and Release Sites

# ACKNOWLEDGEMENTS

    We wish to thank Bob Barber, Gary Clawson, Todd Fredericksen, Mark Johnson, Bob Landis, Barry O'Neill, Diane Papineau, LuRay Parker, Jim Peaco, Lance Peck and Douglas Smith for their help with photographic processes and for allowing us to use their photographs. Our special thanks to Bob Barber for times we have shared in the field.

# PHOTOGRAPH LEGENDS

Photographs are numbered from left to right, then top to bottom.

## Saga of Wolf ~ 9

The saga of Wolf ~ 9 is described on page 2. These photographs document her story and that of some of her pups. They also show the efforts made by project biologists to protect Wolf ~ 9 and her pups.

1. Wolf ~ 9 galloping around the Rose Creek acclimation pen. Photo by Jim Peaco.
2. A pup peers from the pack used to carry it back to Yellowstone. Photo by Jim Peaco.
3. Pups at about three weeks of age. Photo by Douglas Smith.
4. The timid eyes of a pup reflect light out of the artificial den in the acclimation pen. Photo by Douglas Smith.
5. One of the trees blown onto the Rose Creek pen on July 29, 1995. Photo by Douglas Smith.
6. Mike Phillips (Project Leader) and Mark Johnson (Project Veterinarian) check out a pup before release. Photo by Douglas Smith.
7. Douglas Smith places a pup into a backpack for transportation to Yellowstone. Photo by Jim Peaco.
8. Mark Johnson with Wolf ~ 17 before release. Photo by Douglas Smith.

## Quick Identification Chart

The Quick Identification Chart is your means to identify packs and wolves within a pack. It shows each wolf by its general color: black or gray. Project identification numbers are followed by the sex of the wolf indicated as F for female and M for male.

The alpha or dominant wolves are shown as the largest symbol. Other age wolves are indicated by progressively smaller symbols for adults, yearlings, and pups. The pup symbol with 1996 indicates pups were born before this book went to press, but the exact number was not known. The word "Den" indicates that the female of a pack had dug a den, and will hopefully have pups. Wolves that have died are marked with a red "X." Changes between packs are indicated by arrows.

# Year Book

Each wolf pack is represented by one page in the year book. We have included photographs from as many wolves as available. Wolves of the Class of 1996, especially the gray ones, appear similar and identifications have not always been possible.

Maps for the Class of 1995 show the known range of the alpha female and her pack's 1995-96 winter home range as a darker color. Maps for the class of 1996 show the travels of wolves for about the first month after release. For packs that fragmented on release, Chief Joseph and Nez Perce, we have tried to show travels by different wolves by colors and comments on the maps. Maps are inclusive through May 6, 1996.

## Crystal Alpha Pair Cuts One Out

Wolves are Predators! The chase is a way of life. More often than not, wolves test prey and give up the chase when they discover their prey too fit to pursue. In this manner, wolves cull the weakest and oldest animals from the herd. However, survival depends on a successful hunt and this time the wolves' endurance paid off; the chase lasted five minutes from start to finish.

The wolves selected a cow elk perhaps because she appeared slightly slower than the rest of the herd or perhaps they detected a slight limp. Later, while examining her bones, we determined that she had severe arthritis in her right rear leg -- an old injury to the joint maybe.

In any case, once the wolves spotted this cow, they locked onto her and never deviated from their quarry during the chase. All other members of the herd were ignored and soon stopped to watch the chase which continued for another half mile. The wolves repeatedly bit at her throat, never once attempting to hamstring the cow.

A successful hunt guarantees dinner not only for the pack but for many other scavengers. Ravens often arrive before the chase is over.

The painting, Crystal Alpha Pair Cuts One Out, is by Todd Fredericksen. It is a re-creation of a wolf chase by the Crystal Creek Pack on November 13, 1995. The chase was filmed by Bob Landis. Fourteen frames of Bob's 16-mm film are shown around the edges of the page. Two yearlings, probably wolves ~ 2 and ~ 6 actually caught the cow elk.

# People and Events

1. Helicopters were used to capture wolves by shooting (darting) with a needle full of drugs to anesthetize them. Photo by LuRay Parker, Wyoming Game and Fish.
2. Researchers attend a wolf in Canada. Photo by LuRay Parker.
3. Wolves are processed in Canada for shipment to the United States. Note Wolf ~ 13 is visible in upper row. Photo by LuRay Parker.
4. The first wolves arrive in Yellowstone National Park on January 12, 1995. Photo by Diane Papineau.
5. Releasing wolves in Yellowstone National Park. Opening the gate for Wolf ~ 38. Photo by Jim Peaco.
6. Wolf ~ 40 tentatively views its new home. Photo by Jim Peaco.
7. Wolf ~ 40 bolts from its transportation cage. Photo by Jim Peaco.
8. Wolf ~ 39 springs into a new life in a new country. Photo by Jim Peaco.

# People and Events

1. Releasing Wolf ~ 35 at Blacktail Pen in 1996. The electric fence used to keep bison and bears away from the wolf pen is shown. Photo by Jim Peaco.
2. Mule drawn sleds were used to take wolves, food, and personnel into the pens. The quiet nature of the sleds was in concert with no motorized use in the wilderness. Photo by Jim Peaco.
3. A 24-hr guard was kept at wolf pens to keep out not only anyone wishing to harm wolves but also wolf enthusiasts just wanting to see the wolves. However, guard duty was uneventful. Photo by Jim Peaco.
4. Soon after the wolves were released in 1995, the **Clan of Wolf Watchers** lined the road in Lamar Valley to catch a glimpse of their heroes. Photo by Jim Peaco.
5. Rolf Peterson inspects the carcass of a coyote killed by their competitors, the wolves. When coyotes get too close to wolf kills, it can be a fatal attraction. Photo by Douglas Smith.
6. Yellowstone Park Superintendent Mike Finley hosted President Clinton, daughter Chelsea, and her friend Rebecca Kolsky on a visit to the wolf pens. Photo by Douglas Smith.

7. Some wolf events have been sad! Veterinarian Mark Johnson and wolf volunteer J. Douglas Smith take post-mortem samples from Wolf~3 after he was shot near Montana livestock. Photo by Douglas Smith.
8. Wolf Biologist Douglas Smith drags a road-killed deer into the pen to feed the wolves. Photo by Jim Peaco.

## Views From The Field

Generally wolves are seen at a distance, but this does not dull the thrill of the moment as a pack of wolves crosses the landscape. Share here a few of those moments during the last winter in Yellowstone.

1. Rose Creek Pack Cresting the ridge out of Slough Creek. Photo by Bob Barber.
2. Rose Creek Pack near the Lamar River. Photo by Bob Barber.
3. Rose Creek Pack hunting. Wolf~8 is the gray wolf. Photo by Bob Barber.
4. Rose Creek Pack climbing a hill side. Photo by Bob Barber.
5. Rose Creek Pack on the bench south of the Lamar River. Photo by Bob Barber.
6. Two wolves from Rose Creek Pack stalk some elk. Photo by Bob Barber.
7. Rose Creek Pack following the trail of some elk. Photo by Jim Peaco.
8. Crystal Bench Pack at a kill, lower right. Wolf~4 is in center. Photo by Jim Peaco.

# Saga Of Wolf~9

Wolf~9

Pup In Pack

About Three Weeks Old

Artificial Den

Disaster Strikes

About 5.5 Mounths Old

Returning To Yellowstone

Wolf~17

# Class of 1995

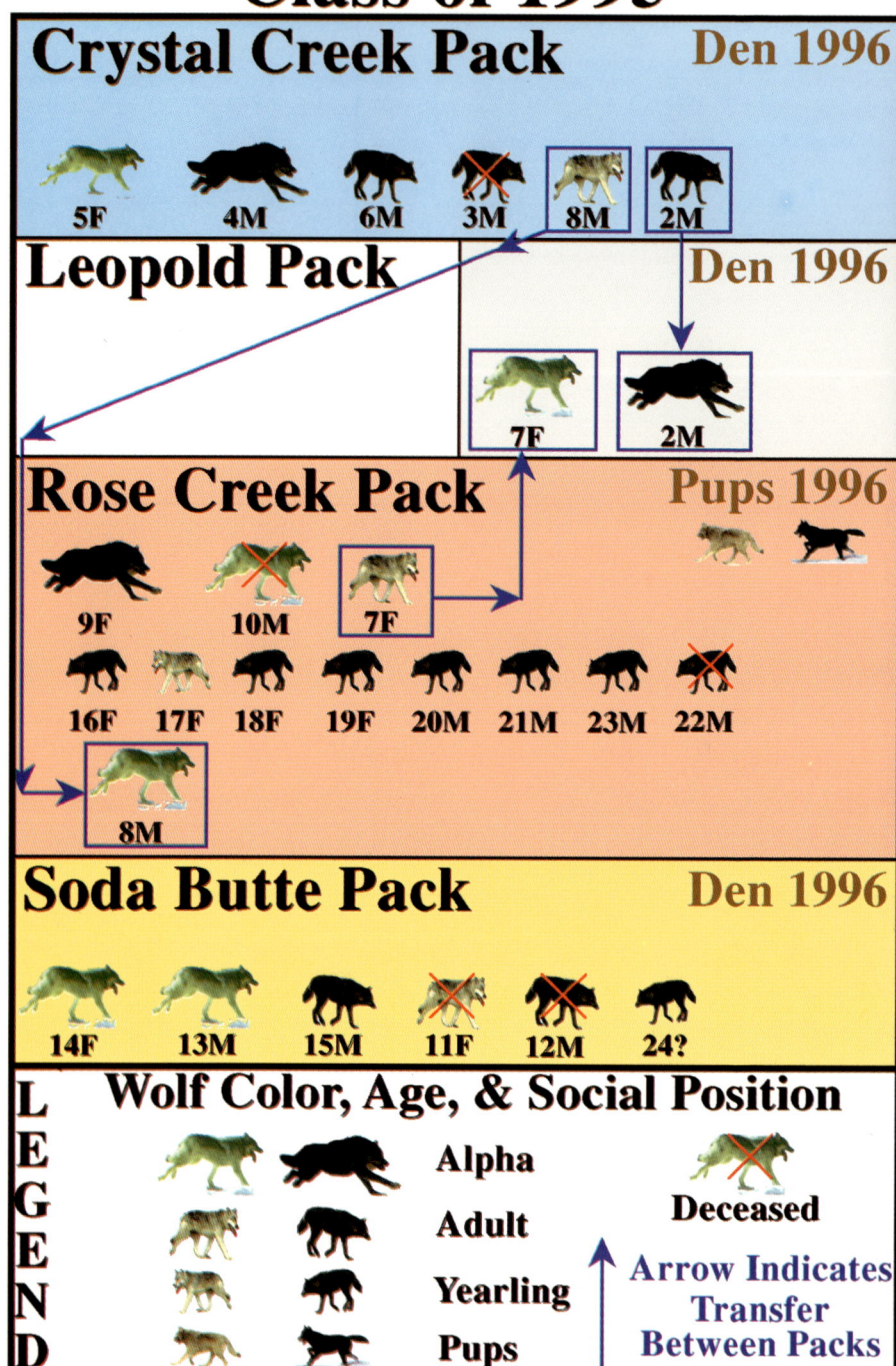

# Class of 1996

## Chief Joseph Pack
### (Crystal Creek Pen)

| 32F | 34M | 31M | 33F |

## Druid Peak Pack
### (Rose Creek Pen)

| 39F | 38M | 40F | 41F | 42F |

## Lone Star Pack
### (Blacktail Pen)

| 36F | 35M |

## Nez Perce Pack
### (Nez Perce Pen)

**Den 1996**

| 27F | 28M | 29M | 30F | 26F | 37F |

## LEGEND — Wolf Color, Age, & Social Position

  Alpha

  Adult

 Yearling

Pups

 Deceased Wolf

# Crystal Creek Pack

Wolf~5 Alpha Female

Wolf~4 Alpha Male

Wolf~9 And Pups Roaming Free

Wolf Pups In Crystal Creek Pen

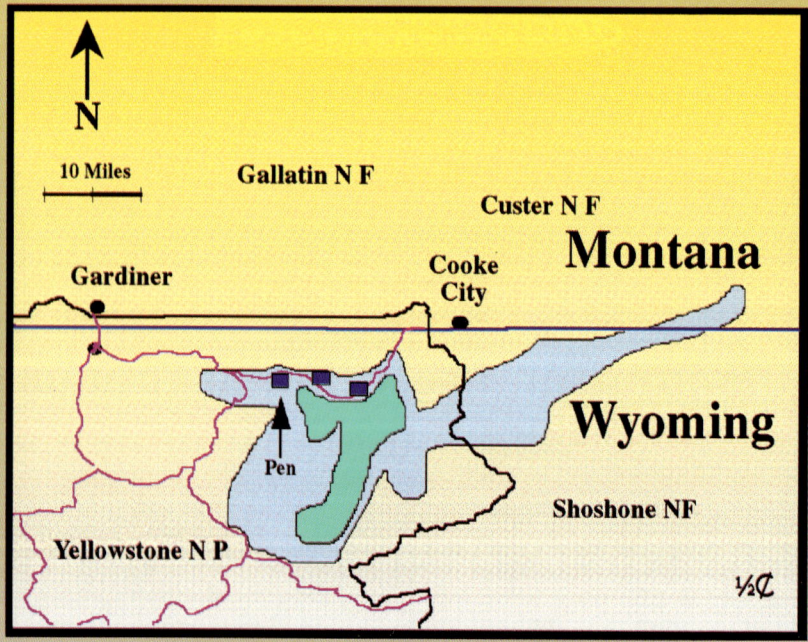

# Leopold Pack

Wolf~7 After Arrival

Wolf~4 Alpha Male

Wolf~7 & Security Box

Wolf~7 And Her Mother Wolf~9

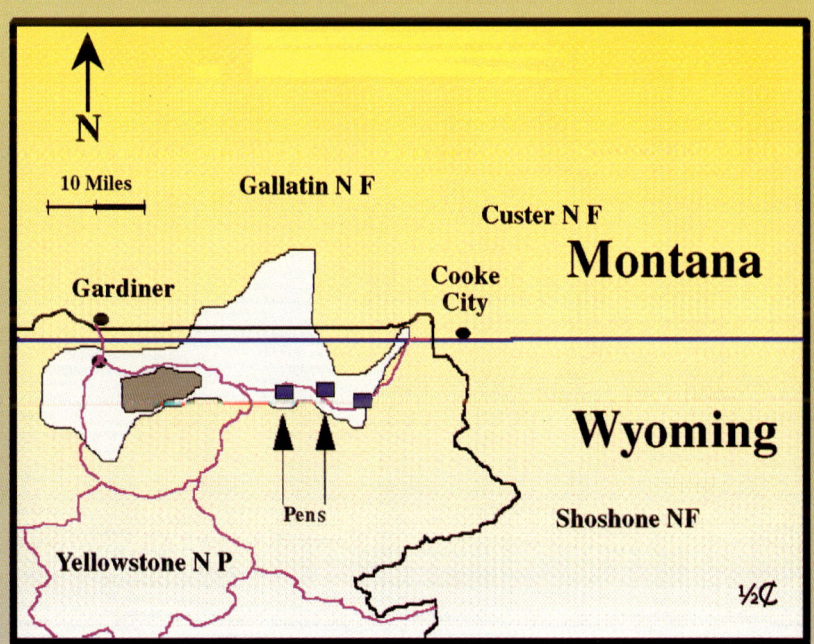

# Rose Creek Pack

Wolf~9 Summer 1995

Wolf~8 Alpha Male

Mom And Dad Lead Pups

Pack Roaming Free March 1996

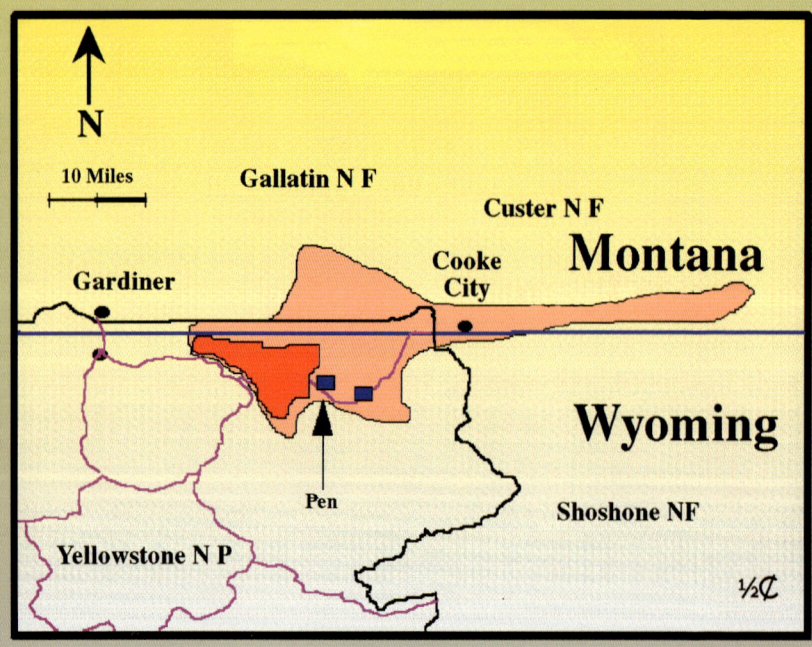

# People And Events

Releasing Wolf~35

Mule Drawn Sled

Wolf Guard

Wolf Watchers

Wolf Killed Coyote

President Clinton Visits The Wolves

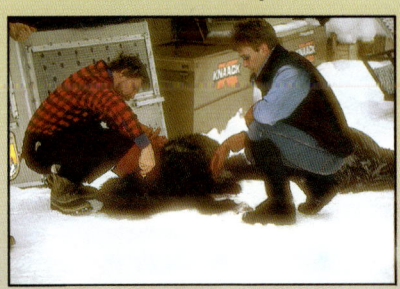
The Loss Of Wolf ~3

Feeding The Wolves →

# Views From The Field

**Leaving Slough Creek**

**Lamar River**

**Wolves On The Hunt**

**Climbing A Hill**

**Lamar River Bench**

**Stalking Elk**

**Following Elk Trails**

**At The Elk Kill**

A combination of characteristics based on the appearance of these two canines will provide the best clues for telling them apart, especially at a distance. The following chart provides a quick "check-off" list for differentiating canines.

Characteristic chart for separating wolves from coyotes.

|  | **Coyote** *Canis latrans* | **Wolf** *Canis lupus* |
| --- | --- | --- |
| Appearance | delicate | massive |
| Color | gray, tan, rust | black, gray, white |
| Ears | long, pointed | short, rounded |
| Muzzle | long, narrow | short, wide, blocky |
| Legs | thin, delicate | thick, large |
| Tail | hangs down mostly | down or out |

In general, **wolves are relatively larger than coyotes** and their bodies appear massive, heads compact. Legs, however, can appear long and lanky, especially during the summer when hair is short. Feet often appear as if flopping when wolves move and the legs move relatively slowly. The legs of coyotes move rapidly, flicking forward and backward.

Comparison drawing of coyote (left) and wolf (right).

**Tail position** offers some help, but is not definitive. The tail of wolves often is level or up, especially if the excitement level is high or the animal is an alpha member of the pack. Coyotes seldom carry their tails as high as wolves do. Red fox, found in Yellowstone, will carry their tails high and often tightly curled. Tight curves are only seen in wolves' tails when they are highly excited.

**Ears** of coyotes are pointed standing high above the head. When coyotes are being submissive the ears are almost horizontal, sticking out to the sides. The ears of wolves appear almost stubby. Coyotes have a long, pointed **muzzle** while that of wolves is short, blocky, and powerfully massive.

Comparison drawing of the heads of a coyote (left) and a wolf (right).

**Color** may be very helpful; black or white canines are wolves. Be careful that shadows don't fool you into thinking that a canine is black when it is not. The light gray of some Yellowstone wolves appears almost white.

Other clues are often found in the field and can be identified to species. Scat and tracks are most often found. Wolves and coyotes tend to defecated repeatedly in the same spots for communication and territorial marking. Massive **scat** piles tend to be made by wolves. If the diameter of the cord of scat is greater than one inch it is probably a wolf. This size criteria works two-thirds of the time.

When interpreting **tracks**, it is important to remember that all wolves were once small and some never develop large feet or tracks. Generally, the large footprints of wolves are distinguishable from coyotes. By the time a wolf is 60 days of age, its tracks, even those of a small female, are larger than those of a coyote. At 60 days, wolf pups are still at a rendezvous site and attended by adults, so their tracks shouldn't be difficult to distinguish from those of coyotes.

Domestic dog tracks are difficult to separate from those made by wolves. Many dogs make tracks as large as those of wolves. Expert trackers use additional clues to identify the maker. Size alone will not do it. Detailed information on scientific methods for distinguishing wolf from dogs tracks is available in slide show or self-study computer disk formats from A Naturalist's World (see Learning about Wolves section).

Front footprint of a large wolf drawn in actual size.

The above wolf track shows a print made by a large wolf. Remember females and young wolves will leave smaller prints, and only an expert can identify small wolf tracks. Take photographs of tracks and show them to an expert for identification.

As a general guideline, footprints (measured without claws) longer than 2.5 inches are not coyote and those longer than 4.25 inches are not dogs. Average sizes for coyote and wolf tracks are given below. These guidelines work about two-thirds of the time. But be careful of using only one clue for identification. Try to find as many clues as possible.

Average measurements of coyote and wolf tracks in inches. The interdigital pad is also known as the heel pad.

|  | Length | Width | Interdigital Pad | |
|---|---|---|---|---|
|  |  |  | Length | Width |
| Coyote | 2.5 | 1.9 | 1.0 | 1.3 |
| Wolf | 4.0 | 3.6 | 1.8 | 2.2 |

**Stride** is a good clue for separating coyotes from wolves. Stride is the distance from where a point on a foot touches the ground to where the same point on the same foot touches the ground again. The average walking stride of a wolf, 53 inches, is distinctly longer than that of a coyote, 24 inches. While the average trotting and galloping strides of

Average strides for gaits of wolves and coyotes (inches).

|  | Walk | Trot | Gallop |
|---|---|---|---|
| Coyote | 24 | 39 | 52 |
| Wolf | 53 | 62 | 91 |

wolves are longer than those of coyotes, there is overlap in the range of values, so trots and gallops are less useful for identifying the trail maker.

# ABOUT WOLVES

This section provides a short overview of the biology of wolves. It includes information on the evolution, taxonomy (scientific naming of species), behavior, and ecology.

First, a bit about scientific names. Species of animals, including wolves, have a single scientific name even though there may be several common names for the species. For example, the mountain lion of Yellowstone is known by over 200 other names including cougar, puma, painter, and panther, but it has only one scientific name, *Felis concolor*. The complete scientific name has two parts: genus and species, similar to a last followed by a first name. Scientific names are italicized and underlined; the generic name is always capitalized. The scientific name of the wolf is *Canis lupus*, that of the coyote, *Canis latrans*. Sometimes we add another name called the subspecies, for example *Canis lupus nubilis* the old name for the buffalo wolf.

## Evolution

Not all biologists agree on how canines evolved, but one scenario postulates the following (chart below). The **clan of *Canis* is old** dating back to the beginning of the Pleistocene Ice Age about 1,800,000 years ago. If you were alive then, you would have recognized dog-like creatures, but they would not have looked like anything we know today. These primitive canines gave rise to two separate lineages or stocks, the red wolf or *rufus* stock and the coyote, *Canis latrans* lineage. The *rufus* stock spread in both the old and new worlds.

In the old world, ***Canis lupus*, the gray wolf,** evolved and its stock gave rise to two lines. One line developed into the small, warm-adapted wolves of southern Eurasia, several of which survive today, but are in serious danger of extinction. The other line became larger to cope with colder, northern climates.

Some gray wolves re entered the new world over land bridges during the Ice Age. Because of the geographic separation, gray wolves later divided into two lines: *Canis lupus lupus* and *C. lupus nubilis*. In the new world five subspecies evolved, including *C. l. arctos, occidentalis, nubilis, baileyi, and lycaon*. In the old world three subspecies evolved *C. l. lupus, communis, and albus*. The subspecies we now recognize had evolved by the end of the Ice Age about 12,000 to 10,000 years ago.

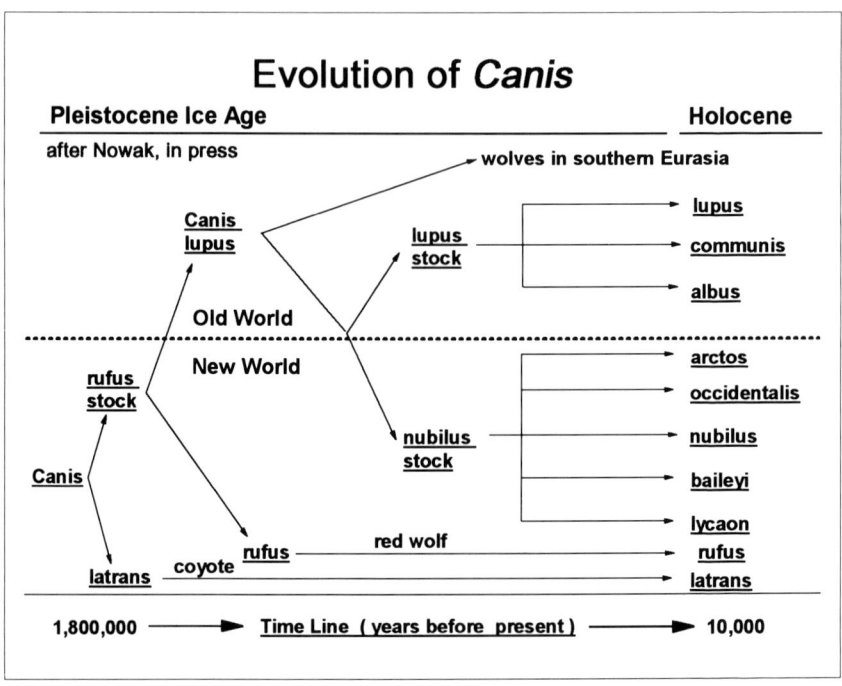

Simplified evolutionary tree for canines (genus *Canis*) from the Ice to present.

## Taxonomy

The distribution of the **five recognized subspecies** of the gray wolf and the distribution of the red wolf are shown on a North America Map below. *Canis lupus arctos* and *C. l. occidentalis* are the larger subspecies and occupy the northern regions of the continent. The other subspecies are small and occupy southern regions. The smaller red wolf, *Canis rufus*, formally occupied the southeastern portion of the United States. Although some have suggested that *C. rufus* is a hybrid between wolves and coyotes, recent studies suggest that the red wolf and coyote diverged long ago and that the red wolf is a separate species.

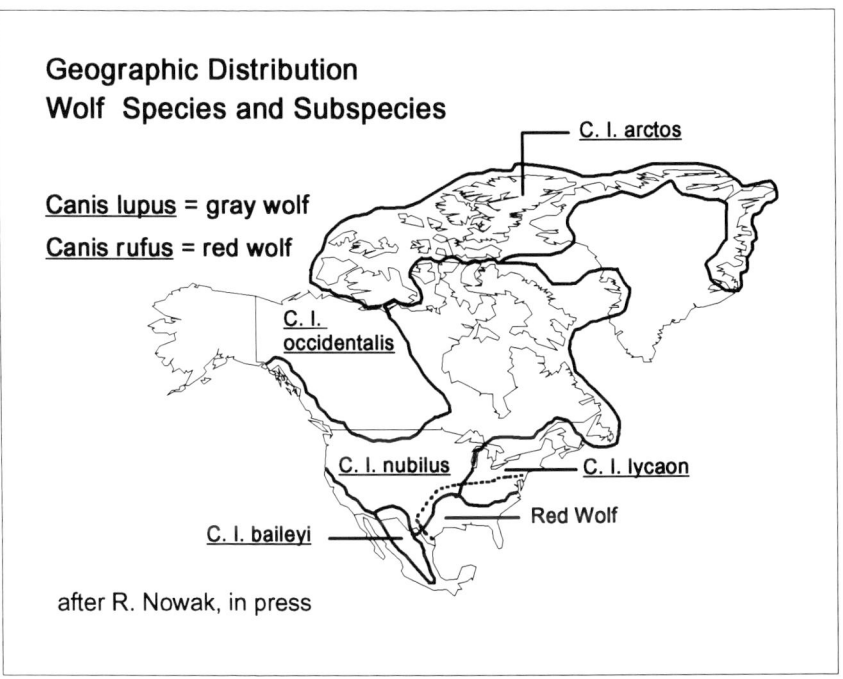

Currently proposed geographic distribution of gray wolf subspecies and the red wolf.

No mention of wolf taxonomy would be complete without considering the large number of subspecies named by earlier biologists. No fewer than 24 separate subspecies were described based on coat color and body sizes. These include the famous **timber, buffalo, and Mexican wolves**, so romanticized in legend and fable.

During the settling of North America, biologists made a name for themselves by discovering animals and naming new species. Therefore, biologists became splitters, listing new species or subspecies based on slight differences. The map below shows the distribution of 24 subspecies of wolves named in North America by early biologists..

Recent studies measuring all the skulls available in museums and private collections suggest that only five subspecies of gray wolves are appropriate. If classification were based on differences in coat color, more subspecies might be recognized. However, coat colors are so variable that they are unreliable for classification.

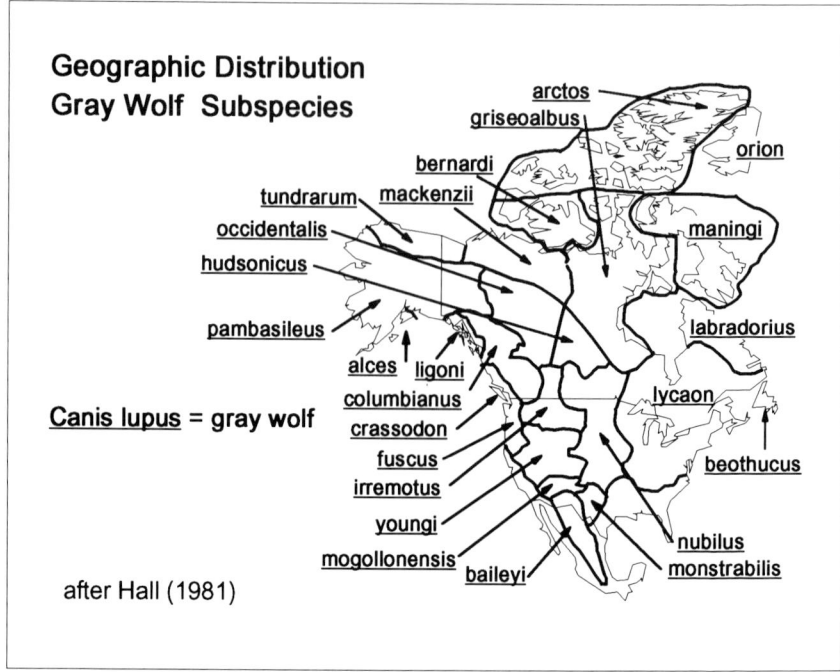

Historical view of the geographic distribution of gray wolf subspecies.

Under the older classification, the subspecies thought to exist in Yellowstone was *C. l. irremotus*. Now, the subspecies originally found in Yellowstone would be classified as *C. l. nubilus* and the translocated wolves would be *C. l. occidentalis*.

## Biology and Ecology

Growing up a wolf is a tough job! There are many things to learn about being part of a social unit - the pack, and there are many dangers to avoid. The life of a predators is difficult and short. A wolf must learn quickly and become self-sufficient at an early age.

Join us now, if you will, to grow up as a wolf. Let me introduce the Wolf Year. The life of wolves can be visualized as a clock face, with each month covering the distance between hour numbers (below).

January is a good month Yellowstone. There are elk to feed on and deepening snows make access to elk easier. Wolves begin reproductive activities early in February. The alpha male spends more time with the alpha female and she becomes receptive to his advances.

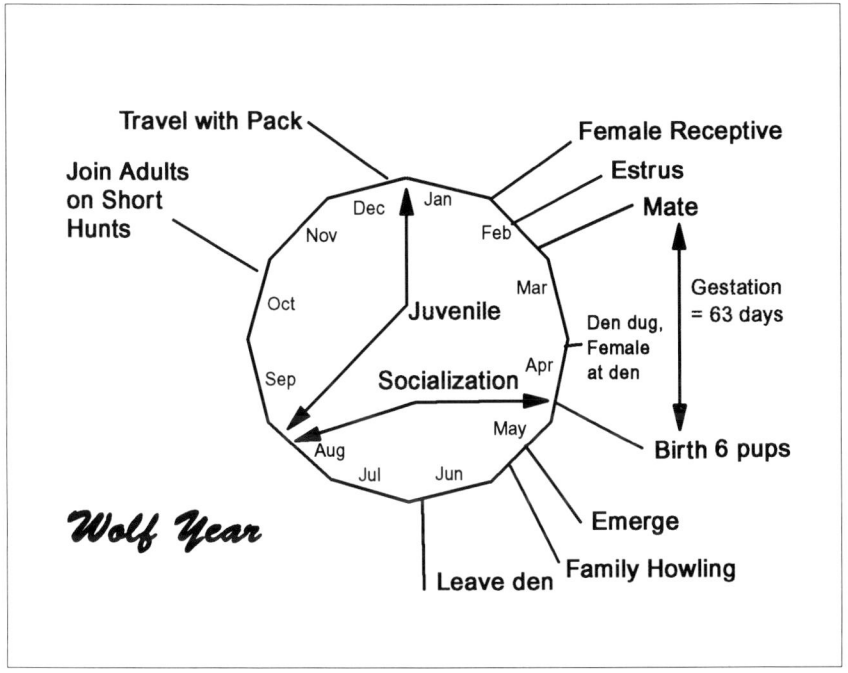

The annual life cycle for wolves depicted as a clock face. Each month may be visualized as the distance between the hour numbers.

The alpha pair increases **territorial activity** including the amount of **double urine scent marking**. To scent mark, an alpha wolf raises a hind leg and urinates as high on prominent objects as possible. Both alpha male and female wolves scent mark by a **raised leg urination**. Placing the urine higher in the air allows its odor to circulate over greater distances proclaiming the alpha pair's status. In general, **subordinates**, either male or female, **squat to urinate** and are not allowed to raise their legs.

About mid-February, earlier in the south, later in the north, the female comes into **heat or estrus**. For about ten days, her urine marks show signs of blood and smell of sexual pheromones. Near the end of the ten-day proestrus period, when her eggs are shed she copulates with the male. A typical **canine tie** between animals occurs and may last up to 15 minutes. Female ~ 9 and Wolf ~ 8 were observed in a tie this year, and female ~ 7 and ~ 2 have left double urine marks. These activities suggest that both packs may produce young in 1996.

**Gestation**, the time from mating to birth, in wolves is 60 ± 3 days. During mid to late April, the female starts to "**localize'**" or stay in one area. The rest of the pack may continue to roam, traveling considerable distance from the female before returning. The alpha female starts digging **dens** and may dig several. In 1995, Wolf ~ 5 dug five dens, but bore no pups. Extra dens serve three purposes: emergency retreats should a den be in danger, clean dens later in the season, and familiarizing pups to more of their home range.

Towards the end of April, **pups are born**, usually six to a litter. At about three weeks of age, the pups emerge from their den. Soon after, they are howling with the family. About the end of June, pups are moved to a **rendezvous site**. The rendezvous site is usually a prominent open area, where pack members socialize and howl together.

From birth to mid-August, pups go through a **socialization phase**, where they learn to be socially responsible members of the pack. From mid-August to the end of the year, pups go through a **juvenile phase** where they begin to learn to be functional hunting wolves.

## Growth and Development

| Age | Development | Weight (lbs) |
|---|---|---|
| Birth | | <1 |
| 11 - 15 days | Eyes open | 4 |
| 20 days | Hearing begins | 7 |
| 21 days | Emergence, Play fight | |
| 35 days | Weaning, Gallop behind adults | 13 |
| 8 - 10 weeks | Abandon Den to Rendezvous site | 15- 22 |
| 16 - 26 weeks | Permanent teeth Winter pellage | 28 - 70 |
| 27 - 32 weeks | Travel with pack | 30 - 80 |
| 52 weeks | Epiphyseal closure | 60 - 100 |
| 95 weeks | Sexual maturity | |

Chart showing the growth and development of wolf pups.

Pups **grow and develop** rapidly. At birth, they weigh less than a pound at birth and their eyes and ears are closed. Their **eyes open** at about two weeks while still deep in the den. After the **ear canals open** at about 20 days the pups emerge from the den weighing seven lbs. They are already **play fighting** to establish their positions in the social dominance hierarchy of the pack.

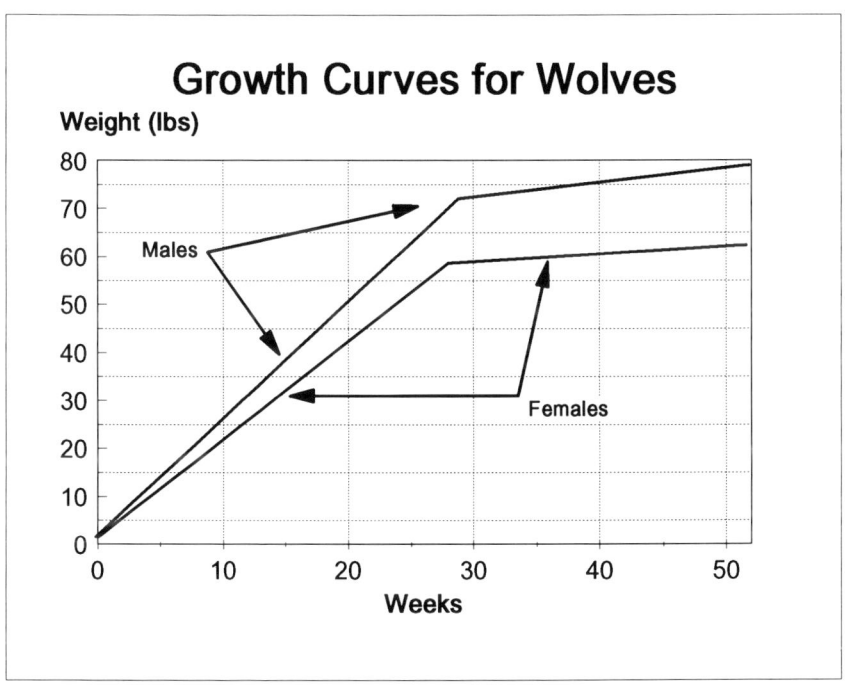

Growth curves for wolf pups raised in captivity.

By five weeks, they have grown to 13 lbs and their mother is **weaning** them. They gallop behind their parents for short distances, and gain the ability to travel. Once they are able to travel, they will be taken to a **rendezvous site.** The trip to the rendezvous occurs at about eight to ten weeks. By this age, males are becoming heavier than females. The **size difference** is obvious. Females may be as small as 15 lbs and males as heavy as 22 lbs.

Around 20 weeks, the pups start getting their **permanent teeth** and develop their first coat for winter. They will need heavy **fur** for Yellowstone's cold. Around 30 weeks, the pups start to travel with the rest of the pack during short **hunting forays.** Males may reach 80 lbs.

At the end of a year, the pups have reached maximum growth. The growth sections (**epiphyseal** tissue) of the bone grow together or close. There can only be small amounts of bone growth after this, but the animals may continue to increase muscle size and body mass. Large males may be 100 lbs at the end of a year, but small females may only be 60 lbs.

At about 22 months, wolves reach **sexual maturity**. Soon after this, they may **disperse** from their pack. Male wolves often disperse as far as 500 miles from their birth places. Females usually do not go as far.

During their first year wolves complete the socialization phase and enter the juvenile phase of growing up. The **socialization phase** includes learning to be part of a pack. Wolf pups must build **bonds** with pack members. Wolves howl together, they wrestle and play, and members returning from their travels are greeted with joyous exuberance. The pups' **diet** is changing from milk to **regurgitated food**. Adults eat food at a kill site and return to the rendezvous site. Pups nuzzle the adults, who regurgitate partially digested food for them to eat. This also helps to build bonds.

## Events of the Socialization Phase

- Social Movement: run, climb, jump, play
- Feeding Behavior Change
- Emotional Bonds for Pack Continuity
- Initiate Dominance Relationships
  - play fighting
  - agnostic behavior
- Predation Behavior

Development stages during the socialization phase as wolves grow up.

Within a week of birth, pups are initiating **dominance relationships** to test who is higher on the social ladder and who is lower. They play, fight, growl, and bite. Pups snarl, grimace, and threaten, behaviors that are known as agonistic. These mock battles and face-offs establish leaders and followers, but most importantly the future alphas or dominants who normally do all the breeding and suppress breeding by subordinates.

Play develops the muscles and coordination necessary for catching and killing prey. Running, climbing, and jumping will later help to capture food, to dodge charging elk, or to avoid larger predators such as the grizzly.

During the **juvenile phase**, which may last nearly two years, pups begin to develop into predators. Wolves must learn to be successful hunters. Those that don't, don't live long. Once pups have tasted meat regurgitated by adults, they learn to eat solid meat. Next, pups have to associate eating with killing. Adult wolves have been observed bringing home wounded prey items for the pups to play with and kill.

---

### Events of the Juvenile Development Phase

- Associate Killing with Eating
- Initiate Killing Behavior
- Limited Mouse Hunting
- Participate in Hunt
  - when to hunt
  - where to hunt
  - how to hunt
- Grow to Adulthood

---

Development stages during the juvenile phase as wolves grow up.

Playing imitates killing behavior. Next, pups start limited mouse hunting including stalking, chasing, and pouncing. Finally, the day comes when the pups join the adults on their first hunt. Perhaps it will only be a rabbit not far from home, but the pups must learn when, where, and how to hunt. They must know when to be quiet, how to stalk silently, when to test herds for weak members, how to recognize weak members, when to chase, and how to kill. It takes time to learn these steps and many hunts fail. Often young wolves would go hungry if it were not for skilled parents. However, even with parents, the wolves may attempt 20 chases before they make a kill.

With a full stomachs, the pups will grow to adulthood, but it is a continual learning process. As they reach sexual maturity, some will chose to leave the pack, hopefully to start their own packs. They may travel 100s of miles before settling into a new area. Others will remain with the pack, to help with future litters. Their loyalty to the alpha pair insures that genes of the parents, which they also carry, will be passed onto future generations.

However, the growing up process is dangerous (see the **survival curve** below). The average life span for a wolf is about six months. While this may seem short, it is because of heavy mortality on wolf pups during their first year. Bears, cougars, and birds of prey may kill pups. Cliffs, diseases, starvation, flood water and river crossings all take their toll. In the wild, only about 20% of wolves live to two years of age. If we consider the survival of wolves that reach two years of age, then the life expectancy is about five years, and some live to ten years of age. A ten year old wolf is very old and unusual in the wild.

Wolves are gregarious animals, living in packs that vary in size from two to 20. Packs may contain non-blood line wolves that have joined from other packs. The **average pack size is five or six** animals. Pack size varies seasonally. During the spring, summer, and fall pack size is at maximum following the birth of the pups. By fall, yearlings and young adults may start to disperse from the pack, decreasing its size. The fourth week of December, 1995, we have called the week of decision as Yellowstone young adult wolves decided it was time to leave the pack and strike out on their own. Numbers 2, 3, and 12 all left their parent packs and started roaming.

Early explorers reported buffalo wolves in packs of as many as 30 animals. Since the extinction of the buffalo wolves, packs exceed a dozen wolves less than 10% of the time. the most common pack size is five or six wolves. If Yellowstone wolves begin to use bison (American

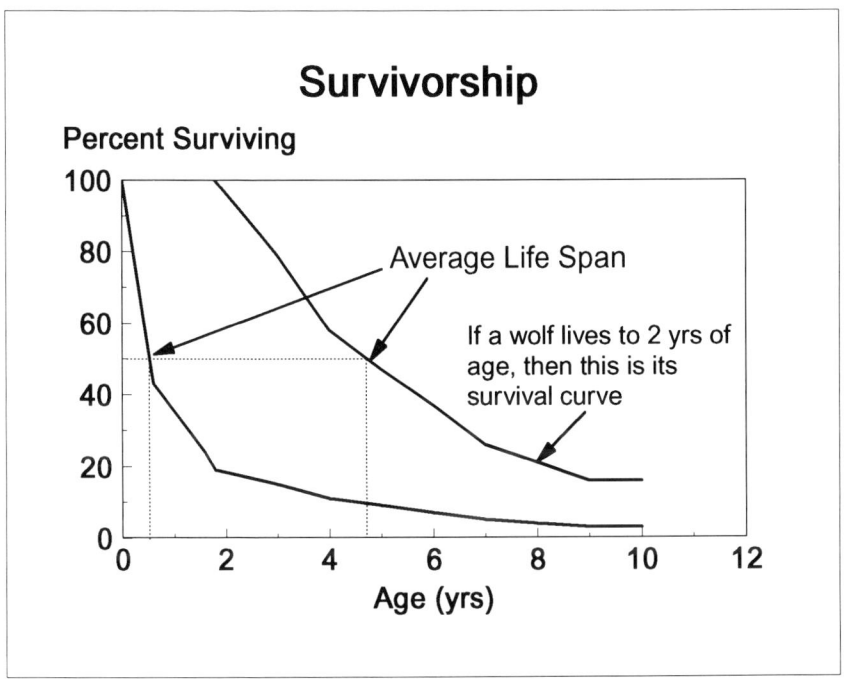

Survivorship curves for wolves starting at birth and two years of age.

buffalo) as a main food item, it will be interesting to see if large packs develop. In Wood Buffalo National Park, Canada, wolves do take bison but the pack sizes are not noticeably larger.

**Home range** is the area traveled by wolves when exploring a region and looking for food. Territory is the area within the home range that is marked and defended by wolves. The home range may vary seasonal and wolves may travel to an area with higher prey densities during winter. Winter territories are critical to the survival of the pack and territory size depends on food availability. In Alaska, where prey is scarce, territories may be 5,000 mi$^2$ and in Minnesota where wolves prey on moose and the abundant deer, territory size is small, about 90 mi$^2$.

While the winter weather in Yellowstone may be very severe, prey density, particularly of elk, is high. Therefore, Yellowstone wolves have been able to have small territories. During the winter of 1995-96, our estimates of home range size were Soda Butte - 250 mi$^2$, Crystal Creek - 70 mi$^2$, Rose Creek - 30 mi$^2$, and Leopold - 7 mi$^2$. Hopefully small home ranges will allow more packs to remain in Yellowstone Park.

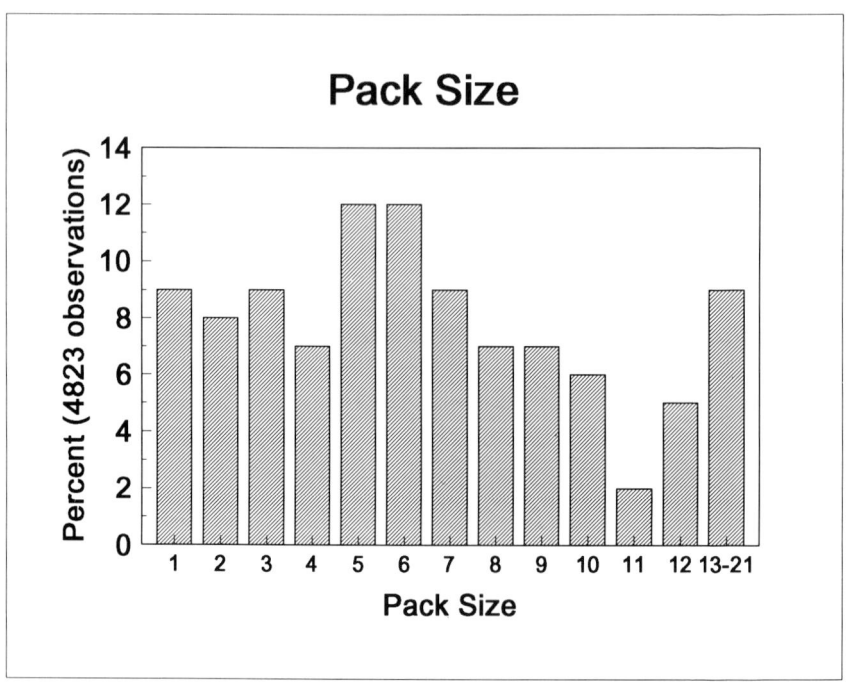

Observed wolf pack sizes in North America over the last 30 years.

## Behavior

Wolves are very expressive in their **behavior** towards other wolves and even their surroundings. Behavior reflects the **social dominance hierarchy** of the pack. The alphas or top male and female are the leaders of pack members of the same sex partners. The next lower members or subordinates of the pack are called betas, then gammas and finally simply subordinates. Each wolf knows its position in the pack, whom it is subordinate to and who is subordinate to it. There is constant testing of the hierarchy, and positions do change. Young sexually mature animals may even leave the pack to form their own packs, as did Wolves ~ 2 and ~ 7, where they can be alphas. Under most situations, only the alphas breed. Subordinates help preserve the pack by helping to raise the pups of the alpha pair.

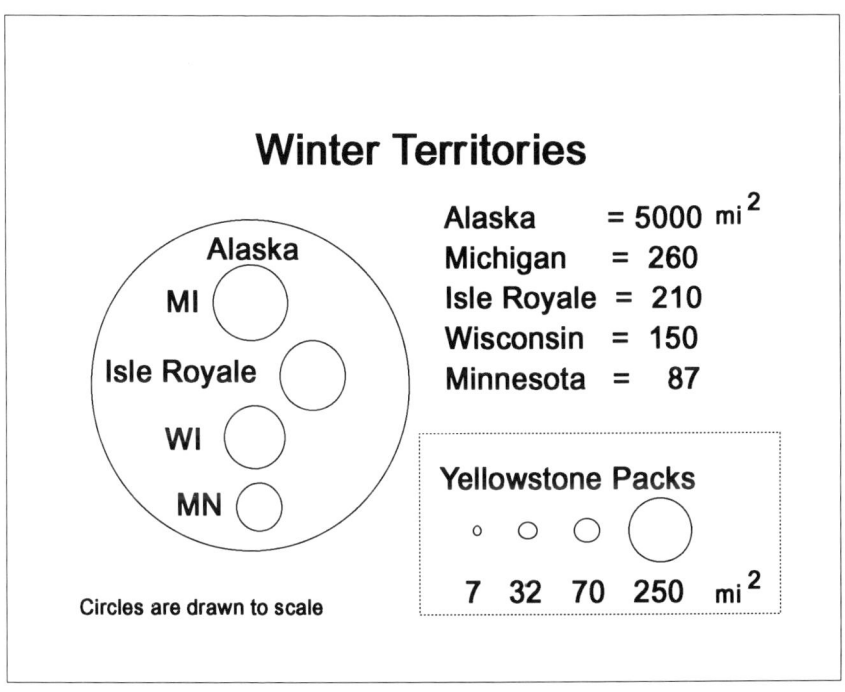

Winter territory size for North American wolves and Class of 1995 packs in Yellowstone.

Wolf watchers can greatly increase their understanding and appreciation of wolves if they know and look for different behaviors. Below is an **ethogram**, a list produced by biologists that includes some possible behaviors of wolves. When watching and taking field notes, codes are used to quickly refer to actions as they take place. Behaviors are grouped by type of social interaction.

To do your own behavioral study, first read the ethogram and see how many behaviors you recognize from observing pet dogs. Learn what to look for in new behaviors. Next, with a pencil and paper at hand, select a wolf to observe; perhaps an alpha or pup. Binoculars or spotting scopes will help. Record behavior codes when your study animal interacts socially. Try to note behaviors of the initiator and the recipient.

| Code | Name | Description |
|---|---|---|
| **ELIMINATION BEHAVIORS** | | |
| DE | Defecation | Rear legs flexed, rump tucked, tail pumping |
| RL | Raised-leg | One rear leg raised, other extended, urinate |
| SU | Stand-urine | Rear legs extended back during urination |
| SQ | Squat-urine | Rear legs flexed, rump close to ground |
| **DISPLAY BEHAVIORS** | | |
| BK | Bark | Loud explosive vocalization |
| SC | Scrape | Legs moved backwards to scratch ground |
| TR | Tail-raise | Tail carried above the horizontal |
| **SEXUAL BEHAVIORS** | | |
| LS | Lordosis | Legs stretched back, back arched |
| MT | Mount | Place chest on back, grasp with legs |
| TA | Tail-avert | Tail to side expose genital area |
| TY | Tie | Copulatory lock, stand rump to rump |
| **NEUTRAL BEHAVIORS** | | |
| FO | Follow | Follow behind another wolf |
| LD | Lead | Wolf departs at a brisk trot |
| LY | Lie | Torso on ground, little movement |
| ST | Stand | Legs extended, little movement |
| SS | Sit | Rump on ground, forelegs extended vertically |
| **OTHER BEHAVIORS** | | |
| AM | Ambush | From stalking, wolf rushes to contact another |
| CH | Chin | Chin placed on back of another wolf |
| OB | Object | Carries or manipulates object |
| RB | Rub | Body is rubbed on an object |
| SN | Sniff | Nose is held near object or partner |

| Code | Name | Description |
|------|------|-------------|
| \multicolumn{3}{c}{AGGRESSIVE BEHAVIORS} |||
| BI | Bite | Jaws closed on opponent, enough to injure |
| CI | Circling | Wolf moves around for opening to bite |
| CS | Chase | Rapid pursuit of fleeing opponent |
| GR | Growl | Rumbling vocalization of low frequency |
| NP | Nip | Jaws close briefly, then head is pulled back |
| PN | Pin | With jaws on opponent, shoves to the ground |
| \multicolumn{3}{c}{SUBMISSIVE BEHAVIORS} |||
| CU | Curl | Shoulder near ground, head twisted to partner |
| LU | Lick-up | Rapid licking movements to partner's |
| RO | Roll | Back on ground, reaches to muzzle of partner |
| \multicolumn{3}{c}{DEFENSIVE BEHAVIORS} |||
| CO | Corner | Wolf retreats to corner to protect rump |
| CR | Cry | High pitched yelp of short duration |
| DC | Crouch | Rump carried near the ground |
| RN | Run | Rapid movement away, no bouncing motion |
| SL | Slink | Head low, tail tucked, wolf retreats |
| TT | Tuck tail | Tail carried between legs |
| \multicolumn{3}{c}{PLAY BEHAVIORS} |||
| BW | Bow | Chest lowered to ground, rump elevated |
| GP | Gape | Jaws held open, no contact |
| LP | Leap | Body catapulted vertically with slight twist |
| MO | Mouth | Jaws grasp, not enough pressure to injure |
| PD | Pedal | Lie on back, legs move touching partner |
| WR | Wrestle | Forelimbs placed on partner's shoulders |

For example, if the alpha male GR (growls) to a subordinate, does it SL (slink)? If your study wolf behaves in a certain way for a long period, perhaps LY (lie), record how long it behaves in that manner. When watching, remember wolves basically sleep, play, sleep, travel, sleep, hunt, and sleep.

# WOLF RESTORATION

## History

Well before the ice melted at the end of the last glaciation about 15,000 to 10,000 years ago, wolves were roaming the Rocky Mountain region. Fossils indicate that two large wolf species of wolves were present: the dire and gray wolves. Heavily built **dire wolves**, Canis dirus, with their massive dentition may have behaved in ways similar to African hyenas. Dire wolves of the Rocky Mountain region were found in Wyoming, Idaho, and Utah, but by about 9,400 years ago they had gone extinct.

Fossils of the lighter built, but equally large **gray wolf**, Canis lupus, have been found in Idaho, Montana, Utah, and Wyoming and date from well before the end of the last Ice Age. Natural Trap Cave east of Yellowstone has yielded fossils that indicate the presence of wolves for over 4,000 years. In Yellowstone, wolf bones were found in Lamar Cave in deposits dating to 1,300 years ago. The fossil record also shows that bison and elk have also been present since the last ice age.

The ecological workings of the wolf / ungulate, predator / prey relationship were established in the Greater Yellowstone Ecosystem 1,000s of years ago. This relationship functioned well until the beginning of the 19th century.

Early trappers and explorers, such as Osborne Russell in 1836 encountered or heard wolves. The earliest reported sighting from Yellowstone came from Henderson who on August 3, 1870 saw wolves in the upper Lamar Valley. Other reports soon followed but regretfully for the wolves, in 1881 Superintendent of Yellowstone, Norris reported that "... the value of their hides and their easy slaughter with strychnine-poisoned carcasses of animals have nearly led to their extinction."

The 1870s was a decade of wolf poisoning that is hard to imagine today. Killing wolves was a "civic duty, done proudly." Again from 1914 to 1926, extensive efforts were made to kill the remaining wolves of Yellowstone and the rest of the United States. In 1915, Congress funded the U.S. Biological Survey to kill all predators on public lands. In Yellowstone, eradication efforts resulted in 136 wolves being killed, including 80 pups (59%).

In the early part of the 20th century, conservationists, including Teddy Roosevelt, were starting to recognize the role of natural predators and to appeal for their protection. The year 1933 marked a turning point in attitudes about predators in national parks. The National Park Service policy was changed to read "... no native predator shall be destroyed on account of its normal utilization of any other park animal..." By 1944, Aldo Leopold had suggested that wolves be reintroduced into Yellowstone. In 1974, wolves were protected under the Endangered Species Act of 1973. The growing realization that wolves were an integral and important part of the ecosystem led to studies about wolf recovery.

The Northern Rocky Mountain Wolf Recovery Plan issued in 1987 proposed restoring wolves to the Yellowstone area. The U.S. Senate appropriated funds to investigate impacts of restoration. In 1990, the first of two reports, Wolves for Yellowstone?, was presented to Congress to answer concerns and problems with restoration. The Secretary of Interior appointed a Wolf Management Committee to develop a wolf reintroduction plan. However, no Congressional action was taken on the Committee's recommendation. In 1991, Congress directed that an environmental impact statement (EIS) be prepared.

The draft EIS was distributed for public review on July 1, 1993. It elicited an unprecedented amount of public comment with over 160,000 responses. After consideration of all comments, the Final EIS was rewritten and released in May of 1994. Secretary of Interior Bruce Babbit approved the Record of Decision on June 15. Rules were developed for the restoration of a non-essential experimental population into the Yellowstone ecosystem. On November 15, the rules were signed by Secretary of the Department of the Interior, George Frampton. With the rules in place, biologists began the process of the actual capture and movement of wolves.

# Process

During the fall in Yellowstone, acclimation pen sites were identified and pens built. A scouting team of biologists went to Canada. They sought Canadian trappers to help locate wolf packs. A wolf from several packs was trapped, radio collared, and then released. This would allow for the rapid relocation of the whole pack when the actual transfer process began. The advance team also secured International, Canadian, and U.S. permits to take the wolves into the U.S.

The day after Thanksgiving, the Farm Bureau filed an injunction to stop the planned move. On December 21, the U.S. District Court heard arguments for the injunction, but on January 3, 1996 the court denied the motion freeing the way to bring the wolves to Yellowstone.

Trapping immediately commenced in Canada. On January 11, 1996, the Farm Bureau requested a temporary stay on the release of the wolves. On January 12, 1996 the first eight wolves arrived in Yellowstone National Park. That afternoon, the stay was lifted and late that night the Crystal Creek and Rose Creek wolves were released into their pens. January 19, six more wolves were brought in and released into the Rose Creek and Soda Butte pens.

Pens were closed until March 21 when the Gate was opened to Crystal Creek pen. On March 22, The Rose Creek pen was opened. That night Wolves ~ 10 and ~ 7 left their pen and **wolves had returned to Yellowstone** after an absence of over 50 years. Crystal Creek wolves were initially reluctant to leave their pen, and on March 23, biologists cut an opening through the back side of the pen. At 9:00 am on March 24, a motion detector indicated that a wolf was outside the pen

The first 11 members of the Class of 1996 arrived on January 23, 1996 and were placed in the Blacktail, Crystal Creek, and Nez Perce pens. January 27, six more wolves arrived and were placed in the Rose Creek and Nez Perce pens.

On April 2, 1996, a panel was removed from the Rose Creek pen where the Druid pack resided. They did not leave their pen until April 12 to 14. When the panel was removed from the Nez Perce pen, the alpha female and her female pups soon left. The males stayed in the pen for two more days. On April 5, the Lone Star pack was transported to their release site north of Lone Star Geyser and set loose. On April 11, the Chief Joseph Pack was transported from Crystal Bench to Nez Perce pen where they were left in an open pen. The next day they were in or near the pen. Additional details of later events in the restoration process may be found in the Chronology section.

# Origins

One of the most critical questions of the restoration process was where to obtain wolves to bring to Yellowstone. Sources were needed where a large number of wolves could be obtained without harming existing populations. Since wolves tend to prey upon species their parents teach them how to kill, a source area was needed where wolves normally hunt elk and bison. Areas in Canada met these criteria, and international cooperation networks were established to facilitate capture, handling, and bringing the wolves to the U.S.

Two areas were finally selected; one near Hinton, Alberta and the other near Fort St. John, British Columbia. Many agencies, trappers, and other local people cooperated to make this process possible.

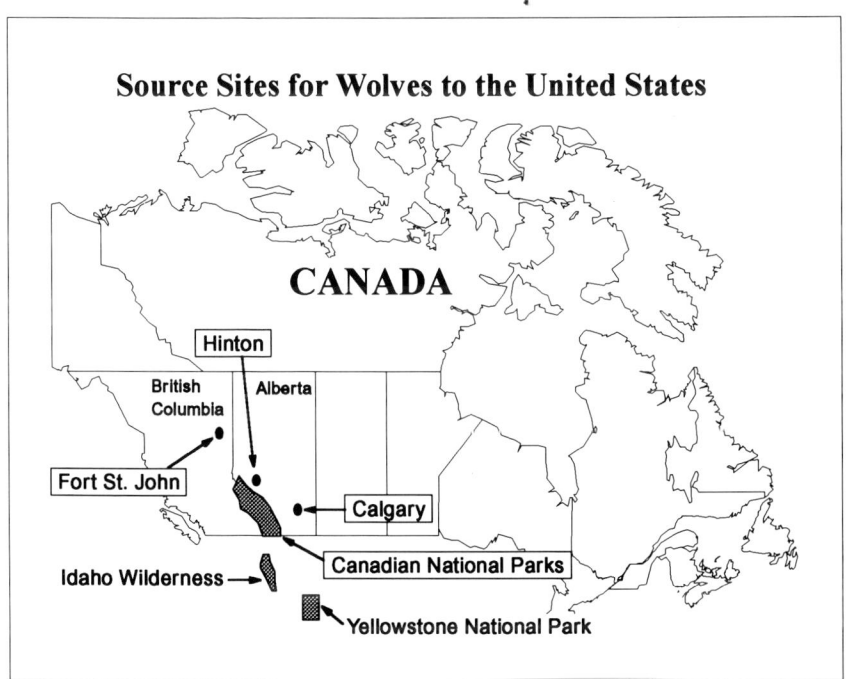

Source sites for wolves in Canada and release sites in the United States.

# Soft and Hard Releases

The science of animal restoration is young, with many unanswered questions about what works best. Questions vary from what causes the least stress on the animals, to how to influence animals to remain in the new locations, to what is most cost efficient. For wolf restoration, two major approaches were tried: soft and hard releases.

Using the hard release process, wolves captured in Canada were transported to Idaho and released as soon as possible. This was a low cost alternative, where duration of confinement stress was reduced. However, wolves unaccustomed to their new surroundings and still "emotionally" bound to their previous home were inclined to wander, and even to try to return home.

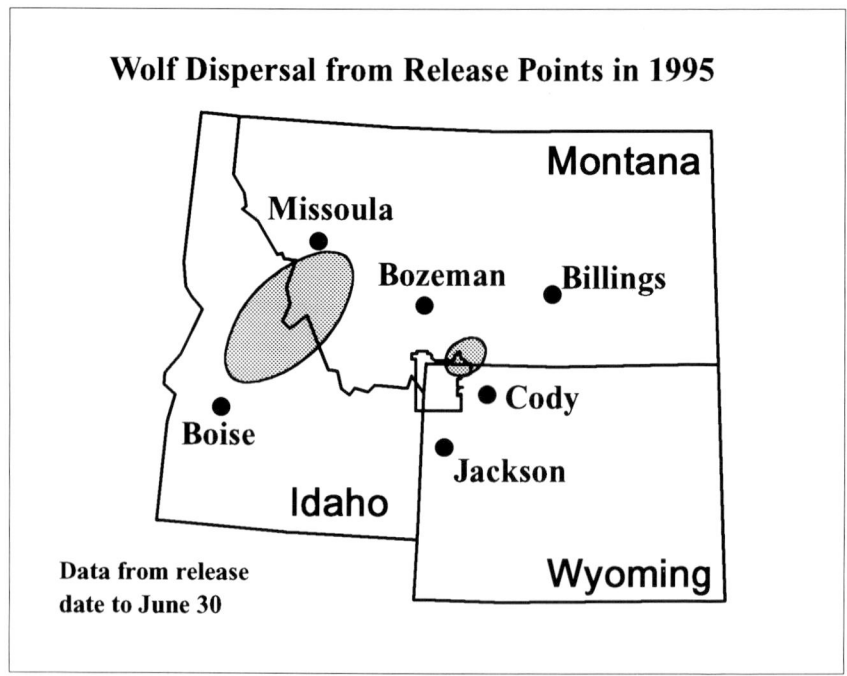

Area where soft and hard released wolves have dispersed.

Under the soft release process, wolves captured in Canada were transported to Yellowstone and placed in acclimation pens for release two to three months later. During confinement, wolves were fed. This alternative had high associated costs and personnel needs, and prolonged confinement. Wolves seemed to adapt quickly and well to the confinement. The longer time, before release, reduced their urge to return home.

In comparison, the Idaho hard release allowed wolves to disperse and become established over a larger area. However, the five packs which formed did not do so early enough to produce young during 1995. The Yellowstone soft release provided pairing in the pen environment, where mating occurred. Pregnant females were less likely to travel, and all packs remained near their release sites. Costs were much higher in Yellowstone, but the number of Yellowstone wolves is already closer to the recovery goal of 100 wolves.

In 1996, combination of soft-hard releases were tried. The Lone Star and Chief Joseph Packs were initially acclimated for two months and then transported to their release sites. It was hoped that this procedure will allow the use of accessible, existing pens to reduce homing instincts while providing release in southern and somewhat more remote areas of the park. Lone Star did not travel far, but the demise of Wolf ~ 36 seems to have caused her mate, Wolf ~ 35, to leave the area. His location is not now known. The Chief Joseph Pack has traveled to the west, out of the park, but its movements have still been less than those of Idaho released wolves. In contrast, the Nez Perce Pack, which appeared to be a tight family unit when captured and was soft-released from it pen, split and has traveled extensively to the north and northeast. It will be interesting to see the extent of their travels when they settle down. Ask a ranger naturalist or at the information desk to learn their current locations.

# Chronology

| | |
|---|---|
| 1850 | Extermination of ungulates and bison in the west |
| 1915 | U.S. Biological Survey began wolf control in west |
| 1925 | Viable wolf populations reported eliminated in west |
| 1926 | Last Yellowstone Wolf Killed |
| 1944 | Wolf reintroduction into YNP recommended by Leopold |
| 1950 | Lone wolves killed in Montana & Idaho in every decade |
| 1972 | Wolf Ecology Project (U of Montana) found no evidence of wolves in YNP |
| 1973 | Endangered Species Act passed, wolves became protected |
| 1974 | Wolf Recovery Team appointed |
| 1978 | <u>Wolves of Yellowstone</u> report said no wolf packs in YNP |
| 1980 | Lone wolf depredation near Big Sandy, MT |
| 1980 | Northern Rocky Mountain Wolf Recovery Plan |
| 1986 | First wolf den in Glacier National Park |
| 1987 | Revised Northern Rocky Mountain Wolf Recovery plan |
| 1988 | Congress empowered Wolves for Yellowstone? Study |
| 1990 | Bill introduced to Congress to Reestablish Wolves |
| 1992 | Estimated 40 wolves in 4 packs in northwestern Montana |
| 1993 | Estimated 45 wolves in 5 packs in Montana |
| 1993 | Draft EIS is prepared |
| 1993 | Analysis of over 160,000 comments from the public |
| 1994 | Estimated 7 breeding pairs (65-70 wolves) in Montana |

**1994**

| | |
|---|---|
| May | Final EIS released |
| Jun 15 | Sec. Interior Bruce Babbit approved the Record of Decision of the EIS |
| Nov 15 | Final rules for nonessential experimental population published in Federal Register |
| Nov 25 | Primary injunction filed by Farm Bureau to stop reintroduction |
| Dec 21 | U.S. District Court in Cheyenne heard arguments for the injunction |

**1995**

| | |
|---|---|
| Jan 3 | Court denied the motion for preliminary injunction |
| Jan 11 | Wolves in transport, Farm Bureau requested a temporary stay to block release |
| Jan 12 | Wolves arrived. Court dissolved stay. Crystal Creek and Rose Creek wolves released into pens |
| Jan 19 | More wolves arrived |

| | |
|---|---|
| Jan 20 | Wolves released into Rose Creek and Soda Butte acclimation pens. |
| Mar 19 | Court denied injunction motions, required radio collars on all wolves |
| Mar 21 | 15:45 Gate opened at the Crystal Creek pen |
| Mar 22 | 16:45 Gate opened at Rose Creek; Wolves ~ 10 & ~ 7 exit |
| Mar 23 | Biologists cut an opening into the Crystal Creek pen |
| Mar 24 | 09:00 motion sensor detected activity outside the Crystal Creek pen |
| Mar 27 | Biologists cut a hole in the Soda Butte pen, wolves detected outside pen on Mar 29 |
| Apr 26 | Mortality signal received from Wolf ~ 10 |
| Apr 27 | Rose Creek female ~ 9 gives birth to 8 pups |
| May 7 | Skinned and beheaded carcass of Wolf ~ 10 found |
| May 15 | Chad McKittrick found with cape and skull of Wolf ~ 10 |
| May 18 | Rose Creek female ~ 9 and 8 pups moved to YNP |
| Jun 16 | Soda Butte pup observed during flight |
| Jul 29 | Windstorm blew a tree onto Rose Creek pen and pups escape |
| Aug 25 | President Clinton visited the Rose Creek pen |
| Oct 11 | Panel removed from the Rose pen. Crystal Creek Male ~ 8 joins Rose Creek female ~ 9 |
| Dec 19 | Rose Creek Pup ~ 22 hit by UPS truck |
| **1996** | |
| Jan 23 | 11 wolves arrive from British Columbia including Chief Joseph, Lone Star, and Nez Perce Packs |
| Jan 25 | Male Wolf ~ 2 seen with Rose female ~ 7 |
| Jan 27 | 6 wolves arrive from British Colombia including Druid Peak Pack and one more for Nez Perce Pack |
| Feb 5 | Wolf ~ 3 killed to stop predation on sheep |
| Feb 11 | Wolf ~ 12 killed southeast of Jackson, WY |
| Mar 30 | Female Wolf ~ 11 shot near Meeteetse by Carl Wall |
| Apr 2 | Panel removed from Druid Peak pen |
| Apr 2 | Nez Perce pen opened, wolves exit |
| Apr 5 | Lone Star pack released at Lone Star Geyser area |
| Apr 11 | Chief Joseph Pack transported to Nez Perce pen |
| Apr 14 | Female Wolf ~ 36 died of hydrothermal burns |
| May 4 | Three pups observed at Rose Creek Pack den site |

# Who's Who in Restoration

This Who's Who serves as both a thanks to those who have driven the wolf recovery process and a listing of current players.

## Government Agencies

**Wolf Reintroduction Administration**
| | |
|---|---|
| Bill Clinton | President, United States of America |
| Bruce Babbitt | Secretary of Interior |
| George Frampton | Asst. Sec. of Interior |
| Roger Kennedy | Director, National Park Service |
| Mollie Beattie | Director, Fish and Wildlife Service |
| Mike Espy | Secretary of Agriculture |
| Jim Baca | Director, Bureau Land Management |

**Rocky Mountain Wolf Reintroduction Program**
| | |
|---|---|
| Ed Bangs | Rocky Mountain Wolf Coordinator, FWS |
| Steve Fritts | Chief Scientist, Capture Program, FWS |
| Joe Fontaine | Montana Wolf Biologist, FWS |
| James Till | Wildlife Biologist, FWS |
| Carter Niemeyer | Animal Damage Control Specialist, USDA |
| William Paul | Animal Damage Control Specialist, USDA |
| George Kelley | Primary Trapper |
| Wade Berry | Primary Trapper |
| Ken Taylor | Darting, Alaska Dept Fish and Game |
| Mark McNay | Darting, Alaska Dept Fish and Game |
| Dave Hunter | Idaho Dept Fish and Game |
| Beth Regher | Alberta Veterinarian |
| Janet Jones | Alberta Veterinarian |
| David Mech | Advisor, National Biological Service |

**Yellowstone National Park Reintroduction**
| | |
|---|---|
| Bill Mott | Former Director of National Park Service |
| Mike Finley | Superintendent, Yellowstone National Park |
| John Varley | Dir., Yellowstone Center Resources (YCR) |
| Wayne Brewster | Deputy Dir., YCR |
| Mike Phillips | Project Leader Yellowstone Wolf Project |
| Doug Smith | Wolf Biologist, Yellowstone Wolf Project |
| Norm Bishop | Resources Interpreter |
| Mark Johnson | Wildlife Veterinarian |
| Terry Kreeger | Veterinarian, Wyoming Game and Fish |

**Northern Rocky Mountain Reintroduction Program**
  Ted Koch         Project Leader, Idaho Field Office, FWS
  Alice Whitelaw    Biologist, FWS
  Valpa Asher      Biologist, FWS
  Mike Jimenez     Nez Perce Tribe
**Red Wolf Reintroduction Program**
  Gary Henry       Project Leader, Red Wolf Project
**Mexican Wolf Reintroduction Program**
  Dave Parsons     Project Leader, Mexican Wolf Restoration
**International Union for Conservation of Nature and Natural Resources (IUCN)**
  World Conservation Union (formerly IUCN)
  Group: Species Survival Commission
   Subgroup: Wolf Specialist Group (WSG)
    Chair and U.S. Representative: David Mech
    U.S. Member - Gary Henry (Red Wolf)
    U.S. Member - David Parsons (Mexican Wolf)
    U.S. Member - Robert Stephenson (Alaska)
**Key Private Organizations**
  Defenders of Wildlife - Hank Fischer
  National Wildlife Federation - Tom France
  National Wildlife Fed - Tom Dougherty
  Wild Sentry - Pat Tucker
  Wildlife Science Center - Peggy Callahan
  Wolf Education and Research Center - Suzanne Laverty
  Wolf Fund - Renee Askins
**Legal Actions**
  Legal Actions Against Recovery
        American Farm Bureau Federation
        Sierra Club Legal Defense Fund
        Urbigkits, Jim and Pat
  Legal System
        William Downes, U.S. District Court, Casper, WY

# FROM YELLOWSTONE RESTORATION LEADER MIKE PHILLIPS

Wolf restoration consists of more than reintroductions. Much work must be done after wolves are released to document the success or failure of releases and the effects of wolves on the ecosystem. Documentation, however, requires long-term, well-conceived studies of wolves and wildlife species affected by wolf restoration. Because Yellowstone's staff and resources are limited, post-release activities must focus on critical aspects of restoration. Accordingly, Park Service biologists developed a restoration program that includes five critical post-release activities that are listed below. These activities are integral components of the Yellowstone Wolf Restoration Program since knowledge gained will allow Park biologists to determine if the reintroductions result in a self-sustaining population.

The five activities require that Park biologists:

1. conduct telemetry flights every fifth day in order to determine wolf survival, mortality, and dispersal; location of dens and rendezvous sites; pack structure, spatial organization, and distribution in response to prey migration; and seasonal patterns of predatory behavior.
2. establish and maintain telemetric contact with all wolf packs and individuals of dispersal age so that other components can be implemented population-wide over an extended period of time.
3. conduct telemetry flights and ground track wolves daily for 30 consecutive days and inspect all known wolf kills during early and late winter to estimate wolf killing rates and prey selection.
4. monitor den sites throughout the whelping and pup-rearing season to document pup survival and adult attendance.
5. establish baseline genetic profiles for translocated and captured wolves

We anticipate that the wolf in Yellowstone will be a keystone predator possessing impressive abilities to reshape ungulate populations, with considerable direct and indirect influences that will ripple through the ecosystem. As the principal stewards of Yellowstone, the National Park Service must play an active role in documenting the effects of the restoration effort. The restoration program outlined above fulfills these obligations. Additionally, the restoration program will allow the Park Service to honor various legal obligations and it will enable and strengthen future partnerships that will lead to long-term studies of other members of Yellowstone's wildlife community.

The five research activities will cost about $100,000 per year. Salaries and logistical support increase the annual budget to $220,000. Unfortunately, Yellowstone Park does not have adequate funds to offset the total cost of the restoration program. To ensure that wolves are successfully restored, Park funds must be augmented with money from non-governmental sources that arise from public/private partnerships.

Wolf restoration is one of the greatest wildlife conservation initiatives in the 20th century. Those interested in the wolves can ensure their existence by providing donations of equipment, time, or money to the restoration program. The organizations listed on the following pages provide you a direct means to do just that. The organizations often have access to matching challenge grants that can be used to increase the size of your gift; you provide the organization with $1 and it is matched with $1 from a challenge grant. Know that you have already contributed to the restoration effort by purchasing this field guide as a portion of the sales profits are donated to the program. With your continued support the howl of the wolf will forever echo through the mountains and valleys of Yellowstone National Park.

Several organizations work on behalf of the wolves of Yellowstone. These organizations are listed on the following pages.

**Yellowstone Wolf Recovery Fund**
**Yellowstone Foundation**
**P.O. Box 117**
**Yellowstone National Park, WY 82190**
**(307) 344-2293**

The Yellowstone Foundation is a non-profit organization that exists to enrich the human experience that is Yellowstone and to increase our understanding of the Park's history and natural systems. The Foundation administers donations made to support Yellowstone wolves.

**Call of the Wild Foundation**
**25958 Genesee Trail Road**
**Unit K-502**
**Golden, CO 80401-5742**
**(303) 526-0811**

Call of the Wild Foundation is a not-for-profit organization dedicated to ensuring the persistence of wolves in Yellowstone Park. The Foundation developed a program that allows you to sponsor a Yellowstone wolf pack. By sponsoring a pack you automatically become a member of the Call of the Wild Foundation and receive their newsletter that provides current and exciting information about the wolves and the restoration effort. The sponsorship kit is ideal for educators interested in sharing the wolf restoration project with students. Profits from the sale of the kit are used to offset the cost of wolf restoration.

**National Park Foundation**
**1101 17th Street NW, Suite 1102**
**Washington, D.C. 20036**
**(202) 785-4500**

The National Park Foundation is a non-profit organization chartered by Congress to receive gifts, manage funds, and help preserve the Nation's natural and historic heritage by providing private sector support to the National Park System. The National Park Foundation will accept donations on behalf of the wolves of Yellowstone. Currently the Foundation is considering awarding a challenge grant to the Yellowstone wolf project so that donated money could be matched 1:1.

**National Fish and Wildlife Foundation**
**1120 Connecticut Avenue, NW**
**Suite 900**
**Washington, D.C. 20036**

The National Fish and Wildlife Foundation provides creative and sustainable solutions for fish, wildlife, and plant conservation, and educates and inspires others to do the same. The Foundation supports conservation activities that pinpoint the root causes of environmental problems, and forges proactive partnerships between the public and private sectors. The Foundation invests in the best possible solutions to conservation problems by awarding challenge grants using federally appropriated funds to match private-sector funds.

**Defenders of Wildlife**
**Northern Rockies Regional Office**
**1534 Mansfield Avenue**
**Missoula, MT 59801**

Defenders of Wildlife is a non-profit national organization dedicated to the conservation of all forms of wildlife. Defenders of Wildlife has created a fund, through donations from members and supporters, of more that $100,000 to compensate ranchers in the northern Rocky Mountains and the southwest for all verified livestock losses to wolves. The goal of the compensation fund is to shift economic responsibility for wolf recovery away from the individual rancher and toward the millions of people who want to see wolf populations restored. When ranchers are alone forced to bear the cost of wolf recovery, it creates animosity and ill will toward the wolf. Such negative attitudes can result in illegal killing of wolves and staunch opposition to wolf recovery.

# LEARNING ABOUT YELLOWSTONE WOLVES

If you would like to learn more about Yellowstone's wolves or wolves in general, classes are taught through organizations listed below. Call or write for their course offerings. Books, videos, and posters below may be ordered from the Yellowstone Association.

**Yellowstone Institute**
(307)-344-2294
PO Box 117
Yellowstone National Park
WY 82190

**Yellowstone Association** for Natural Science, History, & Education, Inc.
(307) 344-2293
Yellowstone National Park, 82190

**Teton Science School**
(307) 733-4765
PO Box 68
Kelly, WY

**International Wolf Center**
(800) 359-9653
1396 Highway 169
Ely, MN 55731-8129

**A Naturalist's World**
PO Box 989-9458
(406) 848
Gardiner, MT 59030

## Of Special Interest

Phillips, M. and D. Smith. Wolves of Yellowstone. Voyageur Press, (612) 430-2210, PO Box 338, Stillwater, MN 55082. Get the inside story from the people closest to Yellowstone Wolf Restoration. Learn about the events, the people, and the wolves! Available October 1996.

Paunovich, R. Documentary on Wolf Restoration. One hour documentary to show this fall, 1996. Ray Paunovish has been on hand and filming from day one. He journeyed to Canada to Idaho to Yellowstone. His eye, and camera, have followed the wolves everywhere. A special treat. Tentative date is November 3, 1996, but check your local listing on the Turner Broadcasting System (TBS).

# Wolves on the Internet

The Wolf Report by Ralph Maughan is an informative home page with the latest on wolf information. Ralph updates his news, often several times a week. The address to reach the Wolf Report is

http://www.greywolf.com/rm/maughan.html

Have fun surfing the internet with the wolves!

The Following wolf educational products are available from the Yellowstone Association (see above).

| | |
|---|---|
| Reintroduction Issue. International Wolf Magazine | $3.00 |
| Looking at the Wolf. Teton Science School. 12 pp | $3.95 |
| Of Wolves and Men. Lopez. 308 pp | $17.00 |
| Society of Wolves. McIntyre. 127 pp. | $29.95 |
| Twilight Hunters. Turbak. 102 pp | $15.95 |
| The Way of the Wolf. Mech. 120 pp | $29.95 |
| Wolf - A Year's Journey. Kosh. 48 pp | $9.95 |
| Wolf Pack. Johnson & Aamodt. 96 pp | $6.95 |
| Wolves. Savage. 159 pp | $20.00 |
| Video: The Wolf. 30-minute | $24.95 |
| Poster: Howling Wolf. Agnew. | $9.50 |
| Poster: I Shall Return. Evanoff | $15.00 |
| Poster: Returning Home. Bryan | $15.00 |
| Poster: NA Wolves, Coyotes, Foxes. LePage | $12.00 |
| Poster: Restoring the Wolf to Yellowstone. Dolack | $25.00 |
| Poster: Winter Lullaby. Geisnes | $150.00 |

# 1997 WATCHER'S GUIDE

Wolf restoration is a dynamic process with changes happening nearly daily. If you would like to receive the **1997** update of **Discovering Yellowstone Wolves: Watcher's Guide**, fill out the form below and send it to us. We will mail you a 1997 copy. You will be billed $9.95 plus $2.00 postage and handling.

## Discovering Yellowstone Wolves Watcher's Guide

| Quantity | Cost (includes postage and handling | Total |
|---|---|---|
|  | $11.95 |  |

Name_____

Phone (will not be used for solicitation)_____

Address_____

Address_____

City_____ State_____ Zip_____

Please inform me when other materials in the Watcher's Guide

series become available:  Yes  No

Please add me to the mailing lists of the Association and Institute:

Yes  No

Mail To:  A Naturalist's World, PO Box 989, Gardiner, MT 59030

**Halfpenny and Thompson**